Can't Keep it to Myself

Rene´ Parson

© 2001 by René Parson

Hannah Communications
P.O. Box 952827
Lake Mary, FL 32795-2827
407-333-3451

ISBN 1-883928-37-0
Printed in the United States of America
LC No: 2001091088

Produced by: Longwood Communications
                    397 Kingslake Drive
                    DeBary, FL 32713
                    386-774-1991
                    longwood@totcon.com

Acknowledgments

Wow! This is simply amazing. You have a desire to complete a project and in the back of your mind you believe in your heart you're doing the right thing. The question is, when will it happen? Finally, frustrated with the issue that has haunted you for years, God has placed people in your life to give you the nudge, the confidence to run, sprint to your calling.

A special thank you to my husband, my best friend, for your tenacious support in my eagerness to seek and obey God's will in my life. We are one.

Thank you to all who took time to review my collected years of thoughts:

Dr. Margaret Duncan
Clarissa Lockett
Carmen Leal
Rhonda Nelson

Thank you to the friends and family members who lent me your ear every time I wanted to talk about my experience as a relative foster parent.

A special thank you to Dana Shafer for the final touches in editing the manuscript.

We must never forget to thank our Lord and Savior, Jesus Christ.

There is no place better than the place you are supposed to be at this time in your life.

Enjoy the Journey.

Table of Contents

Foreword

*But Jesus said, Suffer little children, and for-
bid them not, to come unto me: for of such is
the kingdom of heaven.*

Matthew 19:14 (KJV)

The Bible says, "Train up a child in the way he
should go: and when he is old, he will not depart from it"
(Proverbs 22:6 KJV). In today's fast-paced society, so many
of our children are lost. They are, as the song says, "looking for love in all the wrong places." We hear of school
shootings, gangs, drugs and teen pregnancies. When will
it all stop? How can we save the children?

I consider it a privilege to speak about the author of
this book—a woman whom I can describe in six words:
strong, loving, selfless, prayerful, determined and *coura-
geous.* As you hear her heart in *Can't Keep It to Myself,*
you will undoubtedly see these attributes shining through.
René shares experiences that simply must be told, thus
the title, *Can't Keep It to Myself.* Expect a ride full of
inspiration and enlightenment as you experience the emotional roller coaster of foster parenting.

What sets this book apart from others dealing with
this issue is the rarely discussed aspect of fostering the
children of family members. In actuality this has been
going on for decades; however, relative foster parenting
has not been readily acknowledged, nor has it been served
by resources to strengthen and encourage those who un-
dertake such a task. This book shares the ups and the

downs, the tears and the laughter, the joy and the sadness, the need for true love and the strength for tough love—all in hopes of inspiring and equipping those whom God has called to parent the children of relatives.

René, thank you for having the courage to share some of your life with others, that they might be encouraged, informed and compelled to consider helping the children.

To my wife, whom I love unconditionally, hats off—and a round of applause for a job well done.

Mark Parson

Chapter 1
Start Writing!

"Start writing!" a small voice whispers in my ear. It's nine o'clock on a Friday night—and there's no one beside or behind me. I'm sitting alone in a church pew waiting for my husband, Mark, to finish choir rehearsal. Sensing the Spirit of the Lord, I breathe a quick prayer, and the pen starts rolling.

Life hands out many firsts—first steps, first loves, the first words spoken by an infant. Some firsts are easier to accept than others. For me, life's most challenging first was accepting the fact that my two nephews had come to live with us on a permanent basis. Beginning in 1991, they had stayed with my husband and me for about two years. But this time, it was for good. There was simply nowhere else for the boys to go—except foster care. My heart just couldn't allow such a thing to happen, at least not before trying to help them in any way we could.

Mark and I had grown very close to the boys when they had stayed with us several years before, and we prayed for them constantly. But now they were *here.* What a challenge!

While we felt so alone in our decision to parent my sister's children, we soon learned that we weren't alone at all. Foster care among families is a growing trend in the United States. In fact, in the last decade the number of foster children has grown from 340,000 to 560,000. There are now more than 122,000 children currently waiting for adoption. My prayer is that all adoptive parents and foster parents who take on the responsibility of raising the children of family members will be affirmed for their courage to tackle one of life's most difficult and precious challenges: loving our children.

๗

When Deron and Jeff arrived at our house on the night of June 6, 1997, Mark and I had no idea what to expect. The boys had not stayed with us since 1993—the year they returned to their mother, my sister Monica, who lives in Colorado.

I can clearly remember the day we got the call saying that the boys needed a home. Mark and I hadn't been married a year. When the phone rang, we were in the dining room of our home in Kansas, hanging wallpaper border with soft pastel pictures of seashells. It was my older sister Lisa on the phone.

"René, girl, you will not believe what has happened."

This wasn't the first time that a phone call from family had jarred my peaceful reality. As the youngest of 10 children—three brothers and six sisters—I know a thing or two about family problems. In fact, during this period of my life so much was happening in my family that whenever the phone rang, I found myself leaping to answer it in a numb sort of fear.

"What? What's going on now?" I asked.

"This girl done sent those boys in a taxi with a note to Mr. Goree."

I'm not really sure why my brothers and sisters and I have always called our dad "Mr. Goree." When I asked my sister Lisa about it once, she said it was because he wasn't much of a stay-home dad, so all the kids just called him "Mr. Goree."

My father had read the note from my sister Monica, but did not comprehend what it said. Mr. Goree's life was full of reading with no understanding.

"What did the note say?" I asked Lisa.

"It said that she wasn't able to keep them anymore."

My heart dropped to my feet, and a multitude of emotions flooded my mind. I knew that things had to be really bad for Monica to do what she did—but still, I was angry with her. Today I applaud her, knowing that my sister was only protecting the boys from the damage her life was exposing them to.

Lisa told me that when the taxi pulled up in front of Esther's House of Soul Food—the restaurant my dad had hung out at for as long as I could remember—the boys had gotten out of the cab and run inside. Mr. Goree took the note, read it, and went out to pay the driver.

Anxiously, I fingered another piece of seashell border, knowing that my next question might very well change our lives forever.

"Well, Lisa, what do you guys want to do?"

"We were wondering if you and Mark want to keep the boys, because you have no children and none of us can really keep them."

I turned to Mark, who was standing on a ladder,

hanging on my every word. Though he hadn't heard both sides of the conversation, he knew the song by now and could hum all the parts by heart. After all, this wasn't the first time my sister had decided she couldn't care for her sons. In 1988, she had left them on the steps of Social Services. Deron was six at the time, and his brother, Jeff, was four. That was the year I graduated from college—the year Ma-Dear had passed away.

𝓟

The doctors said it was emphysema that took our Mother Ma-Dear, but I believe it was a broken heart. For years, my mother had struggled, unable to be the wife and mother she thought God had called her to be. Not only did she raise 10 children practically by herself, but she also had helped raise Deron and Jeff—that is, until the day Monica came and took the boys, never to be seen again by our mother for the rest of her sweet life.

I can still recall the day Ma-Dear died. Normally I talked to her every day, but that day I pondered whether or not to call. *I'll call her tonight, after I get home from modeling at the club,* I thought to myself. *But then, I call every morning; maybe I should call her now. No, I'm running late. I'll call later.*

And with that, I was out the door. At that time I was a sales representative for one of the world's finest chocolate companies, Russell Stover. As if my job didn't keep me busy enough, that evening I was to be in a modeling competition held at a nightclub. Soon I would be graduating from modeling school, and I was thrilled at the opportunity to compete. All day long, I dreamed about how I was going to model that night—but the reality of the evening bore little resemblance to my dream! My plan was to model business attire, but believe me, that's not what the men at the nightclub wanted to see! Amid whistles and catcalls, the other women in the contest displayed some of the shapeliest bodies I'd ever seen—in outfits that looked as if they'd been painted on.

Needless to say, I didn't win the contest. And thank God I didn't, because the winner was to become the new model for a liquor company and would appear in all of their advertising. As naïve as I was, I didn't realize what a reputation I would have been carving out for myself, especially as a young, Christian woman.

As I turned the key in my apartment door that night, I felt drained of all energy. But before I could drop my bags and turn on the lights, the phone began to ring. *Who can be calling this late?* I thought to myself.

"Hello, René? It's Lisa. I have some bad news. Ma-Dear died at the hospital."

"What? No one told me she was in the hospital. When did she die?"

"Today!"

"Oh, my goodness! OK, I'll be home tomorrow."

Later that night, I sat in my tiny apartment bathroom, bawling my eyes out and wondering why I hadn't listened to the inner voice that had urged me to call home. Somehow I got myself together and headed for Colorado. *This will be my last trip to Denver*, I thought. *I hope I never see this place again.* My family had been through so many trials that I was just tired of it all. I remembered what Ma-Dear used to tell me all the time: "There's nothing at home but problems." I wished I could just stay away.

℗

We gathered at the home of my oldest brother, Jimmy, to make the funeral arrangements. At some point it occurred to me to ask whether anyone knew where Monica was. No one knew, but they'd placed an ad in the local paper and even called a radio station to have them broadcast a request for Monica to call home as soon as possible. Monica had no idea we would be burying her mother within the next couple of days. *Where could she possibly be?*

"René, you've got the degree in journalism. You write the obituary," ordered Jimmy in elder-brother fashion.

But even a journalism degree couldn't help me conceal the emotion I felt as I labored to memorialize Ma-Dear's life in a few simple words. Raw feeling—the anger and confusion of so many years—spilled out on the paper as I dug deep to express why my mother's life had been the way it was.

℗

"OK, I'm finished," I said to my siblings some hours later. What I had written seemed right to me. At least it was honest and heartfelt. But the reviews from the critics were not so kind!

"Why did you make it so dismal? Ma-Dear's life wasn't filled with that much pain! You make us all look bad."

All I wrote was the truth, I thought, relieved that the discussion was cut short by a knock at the door.

"Oh, my goodness! Girl, where have you been?" Everyone began talking at once.

It was Monica—the boys' mother and my sister. She'd lost so much weight we hardly recognized her. At a glance I knew that in truth I wasn't looking at my sister, but at someone who'd been overtaken by an evil spirit known as *crack*. Tears filled our eyes as we told Monica we loved her and welcomed her into the house. Her hair was wrapped in a dirty blue bandanna, and menstrual blood spotted the back of her pants. We weren't even sure how she got there, as there was no sign of a car. But it really didn't matter. God had brought Monica back to us.

"Where are Deron and Jeff?" I asked her.

"They're with my boyfriend," she replied.

"Well, let's go get them. Are you staying with us tonight?"

"I need to get back."

"Back where?"

"Where I'm staying," she snapped, as if we were putting our nose in her business.

"How did you hear about Ma-Dear?"

"Something told me to read the newspaper."

"But Monica, you never read the paper."

"I know, but for some reason I did this morning."

Back then I didn't know or understand who was putting together the puzzle pieces of our lives, but today I know that God was the One who informed Monica of one of many such family crises—the death of our mother.

Later, my sisters and I took Monica back to the place where she was living.

"Monica, this is where you're staying?" Our eyes took in the rundown three-story apartment building—a crack house. We exchanged nervous glances, and someone voiced the question that was eating at all of us, Where are the boys?

"They may be inside," Monica said as she walked around to the back of the building. "I'll be right back." It was obvious she had something to hide.

The darkness of the night made it difficult to tell much about our surroundings. But we all knew that part of town, and it wasn't a place our sister belonged. As we sat in the car waiting, several lost souls drifted in and out of the house—people looking for love or a reason to live, but searching in a place where these would never be found. *It could easily be me,* my heart spoke truthfully, knowing that one little slip of the mind—too much stress, loss of a loved one, divorce, incident of abuse, loss of a job or of hope—could lead me down the same wrong path.

"What took you so long?" I asked when Monica finally returned to the car.

"They're not here. They're probably over at my boyfriend's mother's house."

"Well, let's go across the street and call her at that store," one of my sisters suggested. "If they're there, we can go get them."

We drove across the street, and Monica went into

the phone booth. It was dark and Monica's back was turned toward us, so we couldn't see her dialing or talking on the phone. When she came back to the car, she told us no one had answered the phone. *She probably didn't even call,* I thought.

My sister Lisa looked back toward the crack house. "Are you sure you want to stay here?" she asked.

"Come and get me tomorrow," said Monica. "I'll be ready when you get here."

"But how can we call you?" Jackie asked.

"Don't worry about it. I'll be ready whenever you get here."

Leaving Monica there was like leaving a part of me. Would we see her again? Our hearts told us we might not. Monica needed help, but there was nothing we could do. We couldn't make her stop using drugs. In fact, it seemed the more we tried to coax her to stop, the more she used.

That night, Monica was our bedtime story. We talked until we could talk no more. *I'm so glad Ma-Dear didn't have to see Monica like that,* I thought as I drew the covers around my chin and tried to fall asleep. Of course, Ma-Dear had known that Monica was on drugs. "That's why your sister ran away with the boys," she'd told us. I just hadn't been able to bring myself to believe it.

ф

The next morning, we got up, dressed, ate breakfast, and once again piled in the car to go get Monica.

All the way there, we feared she wouldn't be home. *She probably feels too ashamed of the life she's chosen,* we agreed. When we reached the apartment, we were all afraid to go in.

My sister Jackie was the brave one. Summoning her courage, she marched right up to the crack house and knocked on the door—lightly at first, then really hard— three loud knocks, as if it were a secret code!

A male voice thundered from inside, "Who's there?"

"You know who this is," Jackie responded in a deep voice.

We all eyed our sister like, *Girl, you are too much!* And then she went inside.

When Jackie returned from her mission, she described for us the inside of the crack house. There was one public bathroom at the end of a long hall. Other than that, the house was filled with mattresses on the floor. It was a place to crash after getting high and nothing more.

"Here comes Monica! Be quiet," said Lisa. "She looks a whole lot better."

"Hi, Monica," I said. "Where are Deron and Jeff?"

"I'll tell you later," she replied.

"Tell us now," I pressed, never dreaming how she would answer.

"I took them to Social Services."

"Where?" Now we were all shouting.

"I'm not able to take care of them" was my sister's only explanation.

We didn't take time to discuss the lies Monica had told us the night before. Instead, we began to search for the boys. We had one day before the funeral, and Deron and Jeff absolutely had to be there. Although they were her grandsons, Ma-Dear had been more like a mom to them—and they were like brothers to me. Good or bad, we were still a family.

Social Services informed us of Deron's and Jeff's new foster parents—a nice white family who owned horses. Although I never met them, I'm still grateful to them for caring for the boys. God's timing is always perfect; we found the boys just in time for the funeral. There, they had a chance to see their mother, whom they hadn't seen in who knows how long.

I eventually came to terms with my feelings about Ma-Dear's obituary. Jimmy and I created words that shared the feelings of all family members.

Obituary

"MA-DEAR"

There were no problems too big or too small for our mother, who was always there in time of need, giving advice and sharing her wisdom, which she knew we needed. That was our mother, the root of our family tree.

Big and great dreams she had for us, yet the little ones she accepted and loved us even more. Her days were filled with many trials and tribulations, but her strong faith and belief in the Lord helped to pull her through each day. It was not easy raising ten children. Even with all the cooking, ironing and cleaning, it didn't seem to bother her the least bit.

We may not have had much, but the love and joy she gave us was more than enough. During the last eight years of her life she was ill with emphysema, but being the strong person she was, it only gave her a stronger will to carry on.

We are relieved that our dear mother has finally climbed over the rough side of the mountain. She has gone on to a better place. She can now rest peacefully.

ℙ

The next year Lisa worked to get the boys back with their mom, who was in and out of rehabilitation centers. The boys stayed with their foster parents throughout the week and spent the weekends with Lisa. In time, Monica was able to prove that she could once again care for her children. But when she got the boys back, it was only for a short time.

Lisa's phone never stopped ringing. It was always Monica—calling from a shelter, a pay phone, or wherever her life of "fun" and escape had taken her. "Things are too bad to handle," our sister would say—and sometimes, "I need help." In the time she had lived apart from her sons, Monica had grown used to the freedom. Eventually, things got so bad that she had to give up the boys again. It wasn't that she didn't love them. It was that she was torn between three loves: her sons, her boyfriend and her drug habit. The boys always seemed to lose.

Chapter 2
The Journey Begins

After much discussion among the family as to who would take on the job of raising Monica's boys, Mark and I quickly decided to do it. Still, my hand was trembling the day I picked up the phone to call my sister Lisa.

"Mark and I will make arrangements to pick up the boys on Saturday," I told her in a voice more confident than my insides felt.

"Now, you know they don't have any clothes," she said.

"That's OK. Just have them ready."

"It's good you guys are coming this weekend. We're giving Jackie a birthday party at the park."

All the way to Denver, Mark and I felt that this must have been God's will and prayed that He would work out the details. Since we had no children of our own, we knew we were in for the learning experience of our lives. A seven- and a nine-year-old would soon be ours to love and care for—overnight!

It was now late July of 1991—my second time back to Denver since the passing of my mother in September, 1988. It was also my first trip home with Mark since our marriage. Mark had met Deron and Jeff before, but I reintroduced them as soon as we arrived in Denver. Mark was more familiar with Deron since I had kept him in 1989 to give my sister a chance to get back on her feet. That summer, Jeff had gone to stay with my oldest sister in Blytheville, Arkansas.

𝔓

We all gathered at the park for Jackie's birthday celebration. Loud music from the '70s and '80s pulsed from the boombox as my brothers and sisters danced to the best of their ability. My dad, Mr. Goree, was so out of it that his head was on the picnic table the entire time. There he was in his late 60s, still getting his groove on. All I could say was "Lord, have mercy," knowing in my heart that only by the grace of God had I been spared from the same destructive influences that had ravaged my loved ones.

It was a cool afternoon and soon started to rain. Storm clouds gathered over our picnic area. We asked the boys if they wanted to go to the mall, so that we could buy them a couple of jackets. Not yet feeling comfortable with us, they bashfully agreed. But pain and confusion filled their eyes.

It was then that it dawned on me what little control Deron and Jeff had over their lives. They had been pushed and shoved into countless situations that no child should have to experience. I imagine all the power they had ever had was the power to dream.

That's why it was little use asking them what they wanted to do. They'd never been given such a choice! For days at a time they had wondered whether they would have a place to live, food to eat—and most of all, a sober mom to comfort and nurture them as all kids need and deserve. I felt so sorry for them, unable to believe that children could be treated so badly.

Soon it was time for us to say our goodbyes and drive off to our new life in Kansas. The fear on the boys' faces spoke volumes as we loaded the car for the long trip. *Where is our mother?* their silent eyes asked. *Why doesn't she want us? Why are we leaving Denver? Was all of this our fault?*

ꝑ

I remember when Monica and I were children and we'd play house. We were the two youngest kids and the best of friends. Monica is in fact two years older than I am, but somehow my aggressive, assertive personality made me the boss!

To me, Monica was the nicest of all my sisters, I guess because we were so close growing up. Just imagine all the fussing and fighting in a house full of seven girls! But Monica was the quiet type—never confrontational, always willing to give. She loved to read and brought home straight A's from school. We often joked that Monica was the way she was because she had been hit by an automobile at age 3!

My oldest brother, Jimmy, was in the front yard working on his car the day it happened. Jimmy was supposed to be watching Monica, the baby, who played nearby on the lawn. But spying her older sisters across the street, Monica somehow managed to open the gate and toddle toward them. In a split second, she was hit by a car—a hit-and-run accident.

Just imagine the impact of a moving vehicle against the tiny frame of a three-year-old! Monica's shoes were knocked off her feet. At the hospital, the doctors diagnosed a blood clot on her brain. My sister was in a coma.

Ma-Dear was devastated. When Jimmy ran into the house to deliver the bad news, she let out a scream of anguish—and with an adrenaline rush that sprang from her fear of losing her baby, she picked up the closest thing to her and threw it. It was a massive console television set.

By the grace of God, Monica gained consciousness, and the first person she recognized was Jimmy. From that day on, she was just like a newborn baby and had to be taught everything all over again.

𝓟

Parenting 10 children was a huge responsibility for Ma-Dear, especially since Mr. Goree did not accept his role as a father. My mother loved my dad until her very last breath—and every day was not a bad day. There was plenty of laughing, joking and playing around. We were a very close family, and even today as the miles separate us, we still care deeply for one another.

As my older brothers and sisters began to grow up and leave home, they helped Ma-Dear out by buying us younger kids clothes and making sure we had food and toys at Christmas. I remember plenty of Christmas Eves when I wondered whether or not Santa would visit our house. In fact, I can still hear the sound of James Brown on our record player, telling Santa Claus to go straight to the ghetto! To my great surprise, the next morning there were presents under the tree. Today I know that it wasn't Santa, but the prayers of Ma-Dear that brought us those presents. I also remember my mother giving our used toys to Goodwill so that other children could have Christmas.

꙳

When my sister Donna got married, she moved to Colorado Springs. With the blessings of Ma-Dear, Monica was allowed to stay with her to help out with the new baby. By this time, Monica and I were in high school. We all saw this arrangement as a good opportunity for Monica; Donna would help out financially and Monica, we hoped, would graduate from high school and go to college.

Monica left home a quiet, innocent teen with a bright future ahead of her. A year later, she returned.

꙳

What in the world is going on? My 15-year-old mind couldn't comprehend what was happening. Slowly, I learned the truth—that something unthinkable had occurred. Monica was pregnant.

Monica was a high school sophomore, and in an instant, her life was turned inside out and upside down. We were too poor for counseling and had too much pride to ask for help. God despises pride, but it lives within each and every one of us. I believe that this period of Monica's life marked the beginning of the low self-esteem and uncared-for feeling that has plagued my sister's life ever since. Because of the shame Ma-Dear feared the circumstances would bring to our family, Monica had an abortion.

Monica never really talked about what had happened. Only the way she lived her life indicated that something had profoundly hurt her—and changed her—deep inside. We attended the same school, but it was as if we were no longer sisters. We had little in common. The crowd she chose to hang out with consisted of the rebels who did things we were taught not to do. Monica began to skip class, stay out all night, and be more and more disobedient at home. This wasn't the sister I used to play with nor the best friend I had cherished.

Eventually, Monica was pregnant again. I was away at junior college when I heard the news. When the time came for the baby to be born, we didn't own a car, so Monica had to take a taxi to the hospital. Donna went with Monica and was there in the cab when Monica gave birth to her first son, Deron.

We hoped that motherhood might bring a sense of stability to Monica's life, and for awhile it did. But before long, she was back to her old ways, and Ma-Dear was left to raise the baby. Two years later, my sister gave birth to her second son, Jeff.

While I was still away at school, my mother's health began to decline. Ma-Dear's emphysema had reached a point where she needed oxygen 24 hours a day. Mr. Goree was still out roaming the streets and had not yet realized that 10 kids were too much for my mother to handle alone. Although I don't remember many days that Ma-Dear wasn't sick, I do remember her peaceful, quiet strength, and I know that the secret of her joy was Jesus Christ.

As far back as I can remember, Ma-Dear believed in Jesus. She would talk to Him and pray throughout the house, and she always kept the television tuned to a Christian station. My mother was a woman with a lot of pride. Her petite figure concealed the fact that she was a person of great strength, with a will as strong as her high cheekbones. That will was the glue that held our family together.

One day during a school break, I came home to find Ma-Dear beside herself because some things were missing. At that time, Monica and the boys were living with her, and we began to suspect that Monica had taken the items. We didn't know what to think when we realized Monica had taken Ma-Dear's Social Security check. *How will she pay the rent?* we wondered. *Why would Monica do this to her?*

Another time Monica told Ma-Dear that if she were not her mom, she would kill her. This wasn't the child my mother had raised. This was a demon-possessed person who would kill for a one-minute high.

Before long, Monica would meet the man who would take her for the ride of her life—ironically, on the highway of death, which is drugs. I often pray for the deliverance of them both.

Chapter 3
Getting Acquainted

It was summer when the boys came to live with us, and the nice weather gave them a chance to become acquainted with Kansas and their new surroundings. In those first few weeks, I often studied the innocent eyes of Deron and Jeff, trying to get a feel for what they were thinking. I've come to believe that children—especially those who've suffered abuse—have a sixth sense about places and people. They always seem to know when certain surroundings should cause their red flags to go up. But that summer we sensed that the boys were breathing a sigh of relief. *Finally, we've found someplace safe,* their faces seemed to say.

Mark and I spent a lot of time making sure the boys understood how much we loved them and their mom—that we weren't trying to take them away, but were instead giving Monica an opportunity to get better. One day, we hoped, they could all be together as a family again.

Deron, the older of the boys and the decision maker of the two, was quite protective of Jeff and his mom. Jeff was very dependent on Deron; rarely did he make a move without a sign of approval from big brother. From my vantage point, as I watched and read their eye contact and body language, it was amazing to see the survival skills they had learned—skills they had mastered in order to keep one another safe. They could talk to each other without saying a word. And when they talked, they knew exactly what to say and when to say it.

In many ways, the boys seemed much younger than their ages. They had to be taught almost everything—how to use silverware, bathe, comb their hair, brush their teeth, and many other things that come naturally for most 7- and 9-year-olds.

For the first two months, Jeff would sleep so much that Mark and I thought something was wrong. And Deron was always wide awake! Night after night, we explained to Deron the importance of getting his sleep. But our words seemed to fall on deaf ears—until one night, when the boys told us a story that tore yet another hole in our already broken hearts.

Many times, they said, Monica would have all-night company after they went to bed. Their mother's boyfriend, whom they called "Dad," would get drunk and wake them up in the middle of the night to do sit-ups and squats against a wall for hours. Rarely would he let them sleep. School was definitely out of the question the following day.

These kids were tired—mentally and physically exhausted.

℘

Signing the boys up for medical assistance was another challenge, and you'd swear I had a plague when I took them in for any type of treatment! One time we had to rush Jeff to the hospital because he couldn't move his neck. His body was simply going through changes, but the doctors suspected he had meningitis, which could have killed him. The boys needed to see a family doctor anyway, since check-ups were required for school. So I took Jeff to a doctor who practiced in a neighborhood around the corner from where Mark and I lived.

Now this was an area where many of the residents hadn't come to grips with the fact that there had been a civil rights movement. In other words, they didn't realize that it was fine for blacks to do business in the neighborhood.

When we walked into the doctor's office, it's likely that neither Jeff nor I looked the part of someone who would carry a Medicaid card.

"Hi, may I help you?"

"I have an appointment to see the doctor"

"OK, just fill out this form, and the doctor will be right with you."

It was a small office with only one physician on staff. I looked around at the people there and noticed that Jeff and I were the only people of color.

"I've completed the form—and here's our Medicaid card," I said to the office assistant. She took the information, and Jeff and I sat down again to wait for the doctor. Minutes passed. Finally, the assistant reappeared and informed us that the doctor would not be able to see us after all. All of a sudden, it seemed he didn't take Medicaid.

Young and inexperienced at this type of thing, I wanted some answers! I pressed the doctor's assistant for an explanation—but then I saw the gray-haired, too-old-to-be-in-practice doctor coming down the hall behind her.

Impulsively, I ran after him, crying out, "What in the world do you mean, denying a child medical assistance?"

He never said a word—just kept on walking. I threatened to call and write every news outlet in the state of Kansas, but it was useless. Angry and dejected, I grabbed Jeff, who looked up at me with eyes full of questions, and stormed out the door.

Too bad we don't all know that when Jesus Christ died, He died for all of us—black, white, yellow and brown. What I've learned is that I must act like Christ all the time, no matter what the circumstances. In trying times like these, when everything in me wants to repay wrong with wrong, I have to call upon the Holy Spirit to help me control my emotions.

During this time, Mark and I were the legal guardians of the boys and had to deal directly with the child welfare system. Having legal guardianship meant that the boys weren't wards of the state; they had simply been given up by their mother. If the boys had been taken from their home by the courts, they would have become wards of the state, and we would have had to become licensed foster parents.

A month or so passed before Deron and Jeff heard from their mom. Hearing the excitement in their voices as they talked to her over the phone made me pray even more that she would get her life together. Monica filled the boys with hope as well, promising them many things she was going to send them and do for them—things I believe she would have done had the drugs not shackled her ability.

As time passed, the boys began to drop their guard with us. They opened up more and seemed to feel safe talking about things they'd been told not to tell anyone— or else.

I'll never forget when Jeff told us about a time when he got really sick while his mother was having a party. He and his brother were asleep on the floor, probably because Monica could not keep furniture; her habit was too costly. In the middle of the night, Jeff woke up vomiting. Hearing the sick child, Monica's boyfriend, Luther, became angry and stuck Jeff's head in the toilet where he had disposed of his illness.

Deron and Jeff also told us of several beatings. Often I've wondered how in the world Monica could have allowed this to happen to her babies. But I've also realized that she was probably too high to care that while she was "enjoying" life, the lives of her children were being stolen.

ℙ

"Whenever Mom would have parties, she'd always send us to the park."

"What would you do at the park?"

"Just play with our friends."

"When would you go home?"

"Not till it got really, really dark. Sometimes we didn't even eat. Mom just told us to go to bed."

The boys were used to being without Monica's love; the tenderness most children crave was something foreign to them. Boyfriends...drugs...anything and everything came between them and their mother. According to her sense of priority, they ranked dead last.

It was hard for Monica to stay in one place. She was always moving from one apartment to another—or from one shelter to another with Deron and Jeff in tow. Monica's motive for keeping the boys wasn't motherly love, but the fact that they were her ticket to a monthly government check and food stamps—benefits the boys themselves rarely enjoyed. When Monica needed a quick high, she'd sell the food stamps along with any food in the freezer. Food that should have gone into the mouths of her kids wasn't too high a price to finance her drug habit.

It's no small wonder that Deron and Jeff had no idea of right and wrong. In the environment they had been reared in, everything was fair game.

❡

Mark and I trusted that our taking the boys in was God's will for both our lives and theirs. We didn't know how long it would last, but we knew we wanted to do our very best. We also knew that with two more mouths to feed, our budget would be tight! No more impulse shopping, seeing a movie whenever we wanted, or eating out when we got the urge to splurge. The amazing thing is that God changed our desires so that what we wanted most was to be obedient to His will. More amazing than that was the fact that through much prayer and a commitment to tithing, our lifestyle hardly changed at all.

Deron and Jeff were not used to eating three meals a day. In fact, the idea of being fed breakfast, lunch and dinner *all in one day* shocked them at first! Sitting down as a family to eat at a dinner table also came as somewhat of a surprise to them; but it became apparent that Deron especially enjoyed these family moments. Even today he likes it when we're all together. He may not admit it, but we can see it on his face.

The boys' adapting skills were miraculous. Whatever the circumstances, they accepted their role and never complained. To many parents, this may sound like a dream come true. But in reality, it was as if they were programmed—like two little robots who never questioned anything, but just did as they were told. Why not? No one had ever listened to what they had to say.

Neither Deron nor Jeff would ever ask for seconds; they always ate just what we gave them. Pleasing others had simply become one of their finely honed skills of survival. This still brings tears to my eyes.

℘

School was and still is challenging for Deron. By the time he came to live with us, he'd passed the age where if he could have mastered the fundamentals, the rest would have come much easier. Unfortunately, those years were spent playing big brother and protector to Jeff. The upside was, these two brothers were stuck together like glue. If you asked Jeff a question, Deron would answer. The love they shared between them was clearly unconditional.

When I imagined Deron at school in Denver before he came to live with us, I pictured his constant preoccupation—not with what the teacher was saying, but with issues that should never concern a child. *Will Jeff and I be able to eat today, other than our school lunch? Will the electricity be on when we get home? Will the phone be working?* Most of all, *will Mom be there when I get home, and if not, when will she come back?*

Deron once confided to me how Luther would make him fight the other kids at school. If he didn't fight, he'd be called bad names and would likely be beaten up himself. I still wonder how in the world the boys made it through those terrible times. It must have been by the grace of God.

Deron's favorite escape from his surroundings was his love for gymnastics. He'd turn flips all day long if he could! Mark and I enrolled him in a gymnastics class, thinking that if one day Deron left us, this experience would always be stored in his memory bank—just as he'd stored the horseback riding he used to do at his foster parents' house.

Deron was in the fourth grade but functioned at a second-grade level. Jeff was one grade behind his normal grade level. To monitor the boys' performance in school, I attended monthly parent/teacher meetings, where the staff often commented how neat the boys looked when they came to school. They were and are two very handsome boys. Both were thin, Deron darker skinned and with a smile to die for, and Jeff lighter skinned, with innocent eyes.

Deron's teachers told me that he didn't talk much in class, which could have been because he didn't understand or didn't want to be there, or perhaps it was a combination of both. We made sure he received extra help though, and Deron survived his first year. I knew he would because Deron is a survivor through and through.

Jeff was like a sponge, so eager to soak in as much as possible. His greatest challenge was pronouncing his words correctly; for example, to Jeff, Mark was "Monk." I attributed this difficulty to the fact that by the time Jeff was two, Monica was hooked on drugs and didn't have time to be "hooked on phonics."

Jeff would take a hug any time he could get one. He was a nervous child, apparently because he had never known where he would end up or if his environment was a safe place to be.

It was hard to hold back the tears when the boys told us how they had often walked with their mother from place to place, bracing themselves against the cold Colorado weather, looking for shelter. Time and again, my mind played the scene of Monica wandering to the nearest shelter, two small boys—clad in threadbare clothes that barely covered their little bodies—clinging to their mother to protect their faces from the icy, winter wind.

So many strange places they had been. The boys would tell us how terrified they were in the shelters— how they would band together with the other children, who also had nowhere else to go.

Jeff had a problem with wetting the bed. We'd often

find his tightly folded wet underwear hidden beneath his clean underclothes. The smell was not nice. When we talked to Jeff about it, he told us that when he'd lived in Colorado, he was afraid to get up in the night. He wasn't allowed to leave his room when his mom had company, so he was never sure when it was safe to come out. The shelters were even more frightening.

𝍏

Even as the boys grew more at home with Mark and me, Deron and Jeff truly missed their mom. Although they never told me, I could see it in their eyes. Mark and I continued to pray for Monica's deliverance.

Because we had no idea if or when Monica would ask us to return the boys to her, our mission was to teach them as much as possible about Jesus Christ. They desperately needed a Christian foundation. They needed to know that God loves everyone, though sometimes we lose our focus and begin looking to the world for happiness— a temporary route to satisfaction. But if we keep our eyes on Christ and know that this place is not our home, then the things of this world become minute. It's then that we can turn our attention to learning how to love one another, just as Jesus commanded us to do:

> *A new commandment I give unto you, That ye love one another; as I have loved you, that ye also love one another. By this shall all men know that ye are my disciples, if ye have love one to another.*

John 13:34-35

What would the world be like if people—all nations and races—really loved one another? When you love, it erases the possibility of abusing little children. It erases poverty and replaces it with a hand-up, not a hand-out. Love wipes out the things that cause hunger in this world. Take a look inside your refrigerator, closet or garage. What good is it really to be wealthy, yet keep all of your wealth to yourself? Imagine how things could be if each one of us had a selfless attitude about our resources—including money, knowledge and the greatest of these things, which is love. God tells us to bring our tithes and offerings into the storehouse and that He will pour out a blessing too big to receive.

Bring ye all the tithes into the storehouse, that there may be meat in mine house, and prove me now herewith, saith the Lord of hosts, if I will not open you the windows of heaven, and pour you out a blessing, that there shall not be room enough to receive it.

Malachi 3:10

I am a living witness to the fact that God's Word is like a blank check. His blessings have known no bounds in my life.

℘

Jeff's ability to excel was breathtaking. Once he began to read, he was a totally different child. When Jeff entered second grade, he was at the bottom of the list when it came to reading, but by the time the school year ended, he was one of the top readers in his class. He absolutely loved to read! In fact, I would often catch him sneaking books into the bathroom to read. It reminded me of my oldest brother, Jimmy, who is very intelligent and always read the newspaper in the bathroom!

As time passed, we grew very close to Deron and Jeff. They became part of the fabric of our daily lives. We invested so much time in their well-being and development that we rarely considered the possibility of their leaving us, at least not at this stage of our relationship.

Mark was serving as a director of the youth choir at our church, and Deron and Jeff joined the choir. Sunday school and church attendance were not a matter of question in our home; we simply went and so did the boys. People at church often commented on how much Deron favored me and Mark. In reality, he looks just like Monica, whom I resemble quite a bit.

On our way home from church, we would always ask the boys what they learned, and they couldn't wait to tell us. We began talking to them about the importance of having Jesus in their lives, and although we believe it's wrong to force a child to accept Jesus Christ as his or her personal Savior, we prayed that one day the Holy Spirit would touch their hearts, and that they would accept Christ of their own free will.

Chapter 4
Hide and Seek

Mark and I never gave the boys free reign in the kitchen. In the morning, I would put out after-school snacks—chips, cookies, and fruit—for when they came home each day at 3:40 p.m. I got off work at 4:00 p.m. and was home fifteen minutes later. I had a fairly stressful job handling workmen's compensation claims, and like everyone else, I often felt I was handling several claims too many—that and trying to raise a family I'd been blessed with overnight!

Around this time, I began to feel an urge to take on the underrated challenge of becoming a full-time housewife. Mark wasn't hesitant about the idea. As a matter of fact, he loved the idea of my being home. Without a job outside the home, I was able to be with the boys when they arrived home from school and devote more time to nurturing both them and my husband. But after about two months, I began to miss the eight-to-five—I think because there was actually less to do at a job outside the home! Eventually I became a substitute teacher, which gave me the freedom to work two or three days a week, yet still accomplish what I needed to at home.

Deron and Jeff were always very quiet. They played quietly and even argued quietly. We often wondered how they acted when we weren't around. Some days they'd beat me home from work, but for the most part I was there when they arrived.

When the boys came home from school, Jeff had a habit of going to the garage to find out if we were home. One day I hid in the closet. Although my car was in the garage, they thought I had left with Mark. Jeff checked the entire house, and once he decided no one was home, the show was on! Without a second thought, he hopped up on my kitchen counter and yelled, "Hey, Deron! I can do anything I want to do and eat whatever I want to eat!"

I couldn't believe what I was seeing or hearing.

"Booty, booty, booty!" Jeff yelled. He must have said that word a hundred times. All I could do was laugh. It was like seeing a totally different kid—one who must have been hiding all of that pent-up emotion deep down inside. You would have laughed too if you'd seen the look on his face when he turned around and realized I'd caught him out of the "good kid" role. His mouth hung open, and he looked as if he'd seen a ghost.

"Come here, Jeff," I said as I pulled him close. Then I told Jeff that I wished he could be himself all the time. It was only much later that I talked to him about getting too rowdy and using foul language that isn't appropriate for little boys.

P

Becoming Christlike was becoming more and more important to Mark and me. We were very involved in our church but had just begun to understand the need to have a real relationship with Jesus Christ. The boys were not used to going to church and really didn't understand who Christ was and what a walk with Him was all about.

Out of their curiosity, they began to ask questions. Mark and I tried to explain the gift of salvation in the simplest way possible. We also made sure that the boys understood the difference between heaven and hell. Deron and Jeff were so young and had adapted to so many changes that the most important thing we felt we could do was to be good Christian role models. This doesn't mean that we were perfect, but our goal was to be like Jesus.

🍷

With the Lord's help, we made it through our first year with the boys. Mark and I had grown closer to Deron and Jeff and felt that they trusted us even more. It hadn't been an easy year; more than once we had questioned whether this task was truly meant for us and hoped that we weren't keeping Monica from fulfilling her God-given responsibility as a mother. We prayed without ceasing that my sister would crave her boys instead of drugs.

But we rarely heard from Monica. In a way I was glad because whenever she called, so many empty promises were made. Mark and I knew she wouldn't be able to keep those promises, but the boys actually glowed.

"I'll send you money for your birthday," she'd say, or, "I'm going to buy you a big Christmas present!" None of these gifts ever materialized. Mark and I decided we would try to make up for the loss by giving the boys their biggest Christmas ever.

Mark's parents are Catholic, so every Christmas Eve we went with them to a midnight mass. That year, we came up with a special plan involving some friends who lived up the street. While we were away on Christmas Eve, our friends would arrange the boys' presents under our tree. We knew what the boys wanted for Christmas. What they didn't know was that we got it all, plus some!

When we left for the service that evening, there was absolutely nothing under the Christmas tree. I'll bet Deron and Jeff didn't think twice about that bare tree since they were so used to being overlooked at Christmas. But we were beside ourselves with anticipation. For once, we wanted the boys to experience the excitement of a Christmas when Santa didn't forget them.

It was well after midnight when we came home from church; the boys were quite tired and ready for bed. Mark and I went up the stairs first, and the boys followed. Then, out of the corner of his eye, Deron spied something through the banister—a gleaming bike under the Christmas tree.

"Santa came! Santa came!" their voices rang out as both boys tore up the steps and ran to the tree, where a bike, a skateboard and other gifts had been lovingly placed just for them. They stood in front of the tree in amazement, not knowing whether they should open the gifts.

Mark and I were every bit as excited as they were. "One or two presents tonight—then we'll open the rest tomorrow," we said, wondering how we'd ever get them to bed. Our plan had worked!

ℙ

Caring for someone else's children can be a tremendous emotional strain. On the one hand, you tell yourself not to become attached because the children are not your own—especially when they belong to a relative. For some odd reason, when the caregiver is a relative, the family members who are not the caregivers seem to feel that they can use both the caregivers and the children much like a yo-yo.

On the other hand, from the natural parent's perspective, there is often much anger toward the caregiver because the caregiver is doing the parent's job. I believe that Monica was upset with us because of an addiction that kept her from being the parent she knew she should have been.

Caregivers are often angry with the natural parent because they don't understand how someone could be so selfish. Many times they can't help but wonder why it seems that women who don't want to care for children have them and keep having them. Relative foster parents make a tremendous investment without control.

Then there are times when you as a caregiver don't understand the kids. Mark and I could never give Deron and Jeff enough love that they would not choose to go back to their mom, no matter how badly she's treated them. There is simply a bond between a mother and her child that's virtually unbreakable. All of the nights they spent in shelters—all of the days without food, lights, water or even shoes for their feet—could never diminish their love for her.

It's like an addiction, this need to receive love from a maternal parent. When the addiction isn't satisfied, the children too need treatment. Just like the addicts who receive substitute drugs like methadone to make it through the day and help curb their appetite for the "real thing," unwanted children need a substitute form of love. That's what relative foster parents provide—a substitute kind of love.

Some addicts learn to live with the substitute, realizing that the "real thing" represents a danger to their health and a deterrent to a positive future. This is the path that Jeff eventually took. Other addicts rebel and adopt an "I don't care" attitude. They act as if nothing in this world matters because nobody loves them anyway—so why should they love anyone or even themselves? Unfortunately, as he grew older, this was Deron's outlook on life.

The caregiver is often poised between the anguish of all of these emotions, crying out to God, *"Why?"*

℘

As Christians, Mark and I learned to lean on the fact that God had chosen us to carry out this unbelievably great task. No matter how tired we got, no matter how often it crossed our minds that their mom might one day return for them, we realized that the boys were in desperate need of love. One look at Deron and Jeff wiped away all our negativity and reminded us of God's ultimate rule: *love!*

I began to get phone calls from my sisters, Lisa and

Carol, informing me that Monica was doing much better and that they thought the boys needed to return home. Mark and I had mixed emotions. We knew the boys' mom had not completed a drug rehabilitation program and could not understand why my sisters felt she was ready to reassume the responsibility of raising her sons.

"Well, René, they're her kids," they said. "Don't you and Mark plan to have your own kids someday? Then you can take care of your own kids!"

Boy, did we hear that a lot! But whether or not Mark and I wanted to have children was not the issue. This was about the growth and development of two emotionally unhealthy boys. Furthermore, Monica's boyfriend, Luther, was now in jail. Mark and I knew this could only mean one thing: Monica needed the boys for financial support. She even had the nerve to call and tell us what we had better do since they were her kids. The bottom line was, Monica needed money, and Deron and Jeff were her ticket to a steady income.

I finally told Monica that if she wanted the boys back, the least she could do was to send for them, especially since she seemed so eager to have them return. There was really no reason why Monica couldn't afford to send for Deron and Jeff. They had been away for nearly two years; she'd had ample time to save for their return.

I was awash in emotion and utter frustration with my sister. *How could someone be so selfish?* Monica had not even sought professional help for her addiction. *And the nerve of my sisters!* They'd made such a fuss and were so adamant about the need for Deron and Jeff to be removed from such horrible surroundings. Now they felt the boys needed to be with their mother. What in the world were they thinking about? Now that the boyfriend was in jail, did *that* make everything all right? No, I reminded myself, *Monica still needs help.*

ℙ

For months, we had barely considered it. Now there was a very real possibility that the boys would soon go back to their mother. Building a Christian foundation for Deron and Jeff always had been important to Mark and me. But now the boys' need to know that God loved them—even when they might think or feel that no one else did—was downright urgent. Many times I had told the boys this since they came to live with us—because deep inside, I always had known they would return. I just didn't know when.

The entire time Deron and Jeff stayed with us, we continued to pray that the Holy Spirit would move on their hearts and that they would freely give their lives to the Lord.

"Hey, you guys! Stop talking," I whispered to the boys one morning in church. "What's going on anyway, Jeff?"

"It's nothing. I just want to go down there," he replied.

"Down where?" I was already anticipating his answer.

"Down there in front of the church," he said.

"Are you sure?"

"Yes," he answered boldly.

"Why?" I asked. Somehow, I had to be sure of his sincerity.

"Because I want to be a Christian."

He said it with conviction. And when it finally happened, we knew it was real because Jeff did it on his own. *Thank You, Holy Spirit!* Tears filled my eyes as I took Jeff's hand and, in support of his decision, walked the aisle with him to the front of the church. Something caught my eye, and when I turned around, there was Deron behind us, saying that he too wanted to become a Christian. Again, my heart jumped for joy!

I knew then that whether they left us or stayed, Deron and Jeff would be able to call upon Jesus for help. I also wanted them to know that God would send His angels to watch over them whenever their mom decided not to come home for two or three days. Although they might not have food to eat or warm clothes to wear, they could be thankful to Him that they were alive. If they could only keep their minds focused on doing the right things in life, I believed they could still grow up to be just fine.

God's timing is absolutely perfect. The boys accepted Jesus Christ just a few weeks prior to returning to their mother. Shortly after they were saved, the phone calls from my sisters became more frequent and intense. We began to feel as if we'd taken the boys against Monica's will, which was never our intent. We had only wanted to help.

Mark and I finally had to sit Deron and Jeff down and explain to them the issues at hand. This wasn't a decision for them to make; they were far too young to understand what was best for them. But we asked them anyway. We knew they would say that they wanted to go back to Denver. What child wouldn't want to be with his mom, no matter what she had put him through? Our hearts' desire was for them to return to a healthy home—a home that truly wanted them.

To our surprise, Jeff, the youngest, made such a profound plea in favor of returning to his mother that we made the decision to let them go. Looking Mark in the eye, Jeff unselfishly expressed what he felt was the perfect reason to return. He said that we had done so much for them; we'd taught them to survive, and we introduced them to Jesus. Maybe if they went home, Monica would have a reason to stay off drugs.

ℙ

Once the boys realized they were really going back to Denver, their old habits returned. They slacked on their schoolwork and acted as if they didn't have to obey Mark or me. In Denver, school attendance was their choice and they had free reign of the house. Monica was rarely around or too high to care. I knew that once they were gone, Deron would return to his old role as protector and decision maker for himself and his brother.

As for Mark and me, we'd have to start life all over again. I was distraught every time I thought about my sisters, especially Monica. Deron and Jeff had been away from her for almost two years, yet during that time, I could count on one hand the number of times she'd called. Had she really gotten any better?

Just as they had come to live with us overnight, the boys left us overnight. Deron and Jeff were too young to travel by themselves, so we sent Monica a round-trip bus ticket to come pick them up. She would come and leave the same day. It was her choice to ride such a long distance, then turn right around without resting, eating or freshening up. It felt as if we were being robbed.

"OK, you guys. We have to pack tonight. Your mom will be here tomorrow. Do you guys remember how to call us collect? Let me hear you say it."

"Zero plus nine, one, three..." they began in unison.

"Good. Now remember, if you forget the number all you have to do is dial zero and tell the operator it's a what?" I drilled.

"Emergency," they said timidly.

"I didn't hear you. It's a what?"

"EMERGENCY!"

"Right. Say it loud so the operator can hear you, OK?"

"OK"

"And what do you say after you tell the operator it's an emergency?"

"We need to speak with our aunt and uncle in Kansas," Deron replied.

"You can't forget my last name or they'll never find me," I said. Both of the boys carried wallets, so I slipped the information inside each wallet with a prayer.

I found myself rattling on like an overanxious parent. "Call if you need anything—and remember, we'll always love you. Whatever you do, don't forget to pray. God will take care of you. It won't be easy, but you are blessed in good times and in bad because God loves you more than anybody in this great big world.

"You may not get three meals a day. You may not be able to wash all the time, but you know how to take good care of your stuff. Remember, it's not how many clothes you have or the brand name that's important, but having something to wear and keeping yourselves clean. Please pray. Pray for your mom. Ask God to strengthen her and take away the desire to do drugs. Now give me a hug."

I held them tight, trying my best to push back the tears. "Help your mom," I continued. "Be good boys and God will continue to bless you. You must go to school every day. It's very important, especially when you don't have any food. Go to school where you can eat. Please, don't sit in that apartment and allow bad things to happen. Learn how to talk. Ask for help. How will anybody know you need help if you don't ask for it? You have nothing to be ashamed of; you're children of God, and you can always come back to Kansas if you need to."

That night, I remember sleeping in Mark's arms the entire night. He was so comforting. He too was sad that the boys were leaving in the morning, but he was also weary from the battle we'd fought with my family to keep Deron and Jeff with us. Mark realized, as I did, that the boys really didn't know what was best for them. They were like a ball on a Ping-Pong™ table. The ball is controlled by the players who swing the paddle, and boy oh boy, can that ball take a beating!

The next day seemed to fly by. Before we knew it, it was time to head to the bus station—time to say goodbye, though we really didn't know how.

"Is everybody ready? Well let's go. The bus should be here shortly." We packed the car, making sure the boys took with them all that they could carry. Though they had to leave behind many of their games and toys, they told us that their mom said she would buy them all new stuff.

We hurried to the station, only to discover that the bus was late. *I wonder if she's even coming,* I thought to myself. *Lisa said she left this morning...*

My mind had barely formed the words when the bus rolled into the station. We watched and waited as every passenger got off the bus.

"There she is!" I blurted with excitement.

Deron's and Jeff's eyes screamed, Yeah! But they didn't say one word.

ꝓ

"Hi, Monica." It was awkward—more difficult than I had ever imagined.

"Hi." She said it half-heartedly. I searched my brain for something to say that would cover the pain of this moment.

"Look at your boys, how they've grown."

"I see," she said.

"Deron, Jeff, hug your mama." I felt as if I were forcing a scene that was not supposed to take place. They were happy to see each other, but no one knew how to express it.

Monica had gained a lot of weight. This was actually a good sign; it meant that she wasn't on crack.

Mark and I hugged her and made small talk about how much the boys looked like her. I looked into Deron's and Jeff's eyes, but I could not read their thoughts as I had done in the past. Perhaps it's because they didn't know what to think.

We had a couple of hours before their departure for Denver; not wanting to wait around at the bus station, we all went over to Mark's parents' house. For some reason Monica didn't want to visit our home. She had no interest in seeing where the boys had lived for nearly two years. Maybe it would have been too much pressure for her to bear.

I introduced my sister to Mark's parents. But like the boys, she barely spoke. Time passed quickly, and we soon made our way back to the bus station. The ride there was painfully quiet. We said our goodbyes, they boarded the bus, and soon the boys were headed back to Denver.

I don't remember whether Mark and I talked on the way home. I felt as if a part of my physical body had been ripped away from me. I also was aware of a strange sense of relief. Raising kids is no easy task.

Mark and I prayed for the boys continually, but several months passed before we had a chance to speak to them. One day I called Miss Esther's café to speak with Mr. Goree, and the boys happened to be there. They came to the telephone but acted as if they didn't want to talk. I told them I loved them anyway and said, "Don't forget to pray!" Mr. Goree told me that they were there to eat.

As I hung up the phone, I couldn't silence the nagging thoughts. *Is this the beginning of another cycle? Is she neglecting them again?*

Chapter 5
Seeing is Believing

Mark and I settled back into being newlyweds. In time, I forgave my sisters and accepted the fact that everything had happened for a reason.

Lisa and I spoke at least once a week, and she brought me up to speed on everything happening at home. She told me that Monica was doing much better; she had a job, and they all seemed happy. I sometimes thought that Lisa told me these things only because she'd been such a strong advocate of returning the boys to their mother. But Mark and I were glad to hear such good news. I didn't care if Monica didn't appreciate what we had done, as long as she took care of the boys and herself. *Maybe she's finally tired of the fast life,* I thought.

As time went on, Lisa and I stayed in contact, and I heard both good and bad reports. The guy Monica was dating was still in jail, and as long as he was in jail, Monica seemed to do better. Mark and I continued to pray.

A year or so passed before Mark and I had reason to visit Denver, this time for the graduation of Donna's oldest son. Seizing our first opportunity to slip away from the family, Mark and I went to look for the place where Deron, Jeff and their mother were living. We hoped the boys would be playing outside the apartment, but they weren't there.

As we turned the corner to go back to Donna's apartment, we spotted them walking down the street with three of their friends. They were on their way to see a movie, so we told them to pile in and we took them to the mall. Monica had just received their check and had given them each $10. It was probably the only share of the money they received.

The ride to the mall felt strange to Mark and me, and probably to the boys as well. They didn't know how to act and neither did we. We could tell that they weren't well kept. Jeff had lost his glasses, and Monica hadn't taken the time to get him a new pair. He squinted so badly that he hardly looked at us. I think both boys were embarrassed by how they looked.

Instead of dropping them off at the movie, we took them to lunch and shopping before the next show. We asked them how things were going, and they told us all the good things their mom was doing and everything she was going to buy them. *Nothing has changed,* we thought. *Their mother has told them just what to say to us.* The funny thing is that the boys seemed happy. Still, before we left them, I reminded them to call if they ever needed anything. They had forgotten our number; I saw no need to give it to them again.

P

We went to Monica's apartment later that evening. She wasn't at home, but the boys were there. The scene was almost too sad to bear—dirty clothes everywhere...no food...only two mattresses on the floor for the boys to sleep on. I couldn't believe my eyes. This was no place for those kids to live.

We asked them where their mom was, and they said

they didn't know. Then we asked Deron and Jeff if they wanted to go back to Kansas. Jeff didn't say a word; Deron looked confused. Tears filled his eyes and mine, and I felt the pain of his indecision. I knew that in his heart he wanted to leave, yet he opted to stay.

How and why my sister chose such a life, I'll never know. I wanted to erase that scene from my mind as fast as I could, but it was impossible. It was clear they needed help, but Monica called all the shots. We were helpless to do anything.

Lisa later told me that the boys once complained about living with Mark and me. They said I was bossy and mean and that Mark and I drank. The fact that Mark and I have never been drinkers did nothing to squelch Lisa's joy in sharing this news. It was as if she took pleasure in catching me not practicing what I preached.

I just didn't understand why the boys would have said such things when all we had given them was love. My only conclusion was that Deron and Jeff wanted to make us look bad so that their mom could feel good. They didn't want her to think they were happier with us. These were simply neglected children who would do anything to get attention from their mom.

φ

Over the next two years, we talked to the boys once or twice. By now they were approaching their teens. Monica's boyfriend had gotten out of jail, and the two of them were back to their old habits. Lisa said she rarely heard from Monica. We figured she didn't want the family to know she was doing drugs again. I often wrote Monica, encouraging her to be strong for the sake of Deron and Jeff. Lisa said whenever she visited their apartment, there was no food and things were a mess. My sisters eventually had the nerve to tell me that the boys should never have left me. *That's how family will do you,* I murmured to myself. *They'll drive you crazy.*

We began to get worse reports about the boys' living situation. Mark and I always prayed, asking God to send His angels to watch over and keep them. But every night, I'd go to bed anxious about their well-being, and often I would dream...

> *At first all I can see are shadows—shadowy figures in the midst of a great darkness. My eyes search the darkness. Then, clearly, I see Deron's face. As the shadows become human forms, I see that Deron is with two other boys, all on bikes, cautiously approaching a parked car. Now the pace quickens as the action seems to lurch into fast-forward. There's a gun—yes, Deron's pointing the gun! Slowly it dawns on me: Deron and his friends are going to rob—perhaps even kill—whoever is in that car. But suddenly, I can no longer see. The shadows disappear and fade to black.*

Panic stricken, I awoke in tears, asking again for God to keep the boys safe and help them make good decisions.

No matter how far away Deron and Jeff were, I had a strong attachment to them; I needed to know how they were doing. It also seemed important that Mark and I continue the process of rebuilding our lives. Mark was very active in our church, and we were both sharp on church attendance. But we had never taken time to study God's Word and learn more about what He expects of us. Mark suggested that we begin meeting with two couples from our church who were more grounded in the Word than we were. The couples graciously accepted our invitation to have a weekly Bible study, which would meet every Friday in one of our homes.

God's timing was perfect, for it was through this Bible study that Mark and I were prepared for the events that soon came. In fact, I can say that this study was the best thing that has ever happened to me. As the saying goes, I'm not where I want to be, but thank God I'm not where I used to be! My relationship with Jesus has allowed me to let go of a lot of baggage. I've learned how to focus on eternal life.

I used to think that I wanted to be this or that, or have big things in life because we grew up so poor. There were times in my childhood when we had no electricity and very little food to eat. There were months when we couldn't pay the rent. We children would sit quietly while the "rent man" placed an eviction notice on our door. Our only hope was that Mr. Goree would come home willing to share some of his gambling money with his own family.

When I made the decision to really "let go and let God," the Lord began to amaze me with His blessings—

not just material things, but the peace He always gives me in the midst of trials and confusion. His armor protects me from the dangers of this world. His angels show up right on time.

Once when I was in college, I decided to stay at school for the summer and work not one, but two jobs. There was little for me to do in Denver, and it put my mother at ease when I was away from all the troubles at home. I didn't have a car or a bike, so I had to walk or ride the bus everywhere I went. Some nights I'd get off work well after midnight. Since this was a small college town in Kansas, bus service didn't run all night as it did at home. My only ride home was the soles of my shoes.

One late night after working at an answering service, I started my usual trek home. It was very dark. As I passed a heavily treed area, I noticed someone sitting in an old car. I could tell he was watching me.

Night after night, I had passed the same spot—perhaps even the same car—and never before had I felt such an eerie feeling. I began to walk faster, almost a slow jog. I could hear each step I made, the pounding of my heart—and then, the start of an engine. Out of the corner of my eye, I saw the car begin to move, keeping pace with me on the opposite side of the street. As I picked up speed, so did he.

I approached a corner where I needed to turn, calculating the speed of the car. If I made the turn for home, he'd surely overtake me. By now my slow jog had become a sprint. I was running for my life.

When I turned the corner, literally out of nowhere, the flashing red lights of a police car appeared. I saw the cop get out of the car—a white gentleman with curly blond hair. He stood in my path, facing me, but I was so scared that I kept on running—right past him and up the hill, through a wooded area and to my apartment. It was only after I had locked the door behind me that it crossed my mind: He must have been an angel!

Thinking back, I've realized that the man in the car had to have watched me walk home night after night. What amazes me now is that I continued to walk that route even after the incident, acting as if it had never happened. Sometimes God keeps us in spite of our ignorance. What a reason to praise Him!

Make a joyful noise unto the Lord, all ye lands.
Serve the Lord with gladness: come before his
presence with singing.
Know ye that the Lord he is God: it is he that
hath made us, and not we ourselves;
we are his people, and the sheep of his pasture.
Enter into his gates with thanksgiving, and into
his courts with praise:
be thankful unto him, and bless his name.
For the Lord is good; his mercy is everlasting;
and his truth endureth to all generations.
Psalm 100

𝔓

During this time Mark started a position with a new company, and we purchased a home. As we grew closer to the Lord, our love for each other also blossomed.

For Deron and Jeff, the chaos of life steadily increased, and Lisa began to worry more about their surroundings. The boys were getting older, and we knew the clock was ticking. Before long, it would be too late to stop them from becoming victims of their troubled environment.

Mark and I had made up our minds not to take them in again. The decision seemed settled, and it gave us a measure of peace. Yet we always concluded the conversation with a caveat: "If we did take the boys back, they would have to stay with us until they turned 18."

Chapter 6
Thursday Nights

For a year or more, our Friday night Bible studies were the highlight of our lives. Mark and I grew stronger in the Lord, enjoying an intimacy with Him and each other we had never known before. Life was full, but the time had come to be tested.

I was on the phone with a friend when Mark came down the stairs with a peculiar look on his face. At first his words made no sense to me. "I can't move my arm," he said. His speech was slurred and confused. As my eyes caught his, I saw that his face was strangely twisted. My husband was having a stroke.

I rushed Mark to the hospital, where he would remain for a couple of weeks. I immediately cancelled a trip we had planned to Denver. My aunt had passed away, and we were scheduled to fly out that day for her funeral. She was the last of my mother's five siblings; now they were all at rest.

Mark's physicians warned me that my husband's prognosis was not good.

"Go ahead and start making arrangements," one doctor told me. "He probably won't live."

But one evening, Mark pulled me to his bedside. "I'm going to be OK, René," he said. "The Spirit has told me, 'I'm with you, and I'm going to restore you.' And I believe it!"

I wanted to believe it too. But honestly, I wasn't so

sure. At that moment, it seemed that the Lord was taking everyone I held dear—first my mother, and now my precious husband. *What will I do without you, Mark?* I whispered to his sleeping form. For now, I would simply take each day as it came.

$$\maltese$$

Our second test came on the heels of the first. I had just dashed in from the hospital one January evening, when the phone rang. Planning to grab a few things and head back to the hospital to spend the night with Mark, I hoped the call would be a short one.

"What's up?" I asked. My sister Lisa got right to the point.

"Girl, Monica's in jail," she said. "She didn't even have shoes on when the police picked her up."

"What's she in jail for this time?"

"We don't even know."

"Where are the boys?" That's what concerned me the most.

"We had to go get them from that apartment. Girl, I'm surprised they don't shut down that building. Monica ought to be ashamed of herself. The boys didn't even know she was in jail."

"Why not?"

"Deron had been out all night, and Jeff was at a friend's house. He goes over there to eat," she said.

"Oh, Lord. What's going to happen?" Already numbed by the events of Mark's illness, I could barely brace myself for what came next.

"Well, can you take them?" Lisa asked.

"Lisa, I can't take them! Mark is in the hospital. He can't walk—in fact, they say he'll have to learn to walk all over again! Why can't you guys keep them?" What I wanted to say was that the boys never should have left us in the first place. "And Lisa, you're not talking about us keeping two little boys. These are teenagers now! And if I'm not mistaken, you told me they didn't want to stay with me because they didn't like me. So, no. I don't want to go through all that mess again."

My mouth was working faster than my mind. Before I knew it, I was saying the very things I didn't want to say.

"You never should have made us give them back! Now here you are calling again. Mark and I are not here to be played with! We have lives too. All I heard the last time they were here was how they needed to be with their mama. Now they're with her, so you all keep them."

Having emptied both barrels, I tried to pull myself together. "How long is she supposed to be in jail?"

"We don't know," said Lisa.

"Well, I don't have the money to help get her out. Maybe she needs to stay there and sleep off some of those drugs."

As I hung up the phone, I was gripped by the same anger and frustration that had agonized me for years. Monica's life-style and her selfish attitude never ceased to amaze me. I also was upset with my sisters because they had known this would happen. Until Monica chose to get help, until she chose to quit fighting her battles on her own, nothing would change. Until the cycle was broken, it would spin on and on, out of control—a maelstrom pulling everyone along in its powerful current.

The nerve of them! I thought. *They don't even care about me. They think they can just call up and say "Keep the boys" whenever they want. How do they expect me to take care of two teenage boys and a sick husband too?* Just then, the imaginary conversation in my mind was interrupted by a still, small voice that was not my own.

"René," the voice said, "call Lisa back."

What did I just hear? It came again.

"Call Lisa back and tell her you'll keep the boys."

That time it was so clear that I couldn't question what I'd heard. Some may call it a guilty conscience; I knew it was the Holy Spirit. I picked up the phone to call my sister back.

"Hello, Lisa? This is René. I was out of line and I apologize."

"Girl, you don't have to apologize! I understand."

"No, I know you're the oldest, and I shouldn't talk to you like that. Send the boys if you have to. It would be nice if you could at least keep them until school's out."

"Well, like I said, we don't even know how long she'll be in jail. But even if she does get out, there's no way those boys should have to stay with her. I'm tired, René. This girl is too much. It's time to stop thinking about her and start focusing on the boys."

I agreed wholeheartedly.

"I'm tired of her too, and I know we need to focus on Deron especially. Monica is grown, and we can't make her choose to do right. The boys have been put on the back burner all of their lives. As far as I'm concerned, she can stay in jail. When she's out, we don't know where she is, her kids don't know where she is, and we don't know what she's doing to get drugs. Monica's in prison—whether she's in or out of jail—because she doesn't know what it means to be truly free."

I didn't know whether Lisa truly understood what I was saying. She too depended on her own abilities and had not yet learned to lean on the Lord. (She has since given her life to Jesus Christ.)

"All we can do is pray for Monica," I concluded. "She has to decide how she wants to live the rest of her life. By the way, where is the little guy?" I meant Monica's boyfriend; his name wasn't worth mentioning. "Is he back in jail too?"

"We don't know," said Lisa.

"Well, it's getting late. You guys keep me updated. I have to go now."

As I hung up the phone, a prayer was already on my lips. *Oh, my Lord. What did I just do? That had to be You, Lord, because that's not a decision I would have made. Mark's in the hospital, and dear God, I pray that You'll prepare his heart for this news.*

On my way to the hospital that night, I decided not to share with Mark what I had just discussed with Lisa.

He was already sick; I didn't want to kill him. The news would have to wait.

ჴ

A few weeks passed with no word from Denver, so I called Lisa to find out what was going on.

"Monica's still in jail, and Pooh is keeping Deron," my sister informed me. "Jeff is staying with Larry." Pooh is Lisa's son, and Larry is our second oldest brother.

"Oh, Lisa! Couldn't you or Donna keep Jeff? You know Larry isn't a good influence for him!"

"Now you know Donna is not offering to keep nobody. I'm sick! I can't keep those boys. I keep my own grandson most of the time. Pooh said he and his wife may decide to keep them both."

"That might be better, Lisa," I said, thinking hard. "They need a positive male role model."

"Yeah, but Pooh and Sara are just so young. Two teenagers might be too much."

I mustered up the courage to ask my next question. "Um-hum, Lisa, is Larry doing drugs around Jeff?"

"You know he is," she replied. "And he said Jeff is cramping his style. Deron never wants to do homework, but he really likes Pooh. Pooh said he's teaching him everything. Girl, he's living better than he's ever lived. He has his own room and everything." Lisa said it as if Mark and I hadn't done a thing for the boys. *Family is too much!* I thought. But I didn't say anything, just listened.

"Well, I'm sure Deron appreciates everything," I said

when Lisa stopped talking. "So, you guys will keep them until Monica gets out. And then what?"

"Girl, I don't know." I could tell she was fed up with it all.

"Lisa, look. If they come back, Mark and I want to keep the boys until they graduate from high school. It's not fair for them to be tossed around, separated, and all that other stuff. Please understand that I'm not gonna put up with you all calling us and talking about how they need to be with their mama. They need stability. Having them go back and forth messes with our lives, and most of all, with the boys' lives."

I was on a roll and Lisa seemed to be hearing me, so I took a deep breath and continued.

"The last time they were here, we had to make a lot of adjustments. You have kids! You know that you're basically on a very strict schedule. The days of eating on the run, leaving when you want, the washing, the cleaning—everything changes! I'm not fussing, but I want to make sure everybody understands. It's not as simple as 'Mark and René can take care of the boys' and everything is just fine."

"OK, René," Lisa said. "I don't blame you for making sure that if the boys come, they'll be there till they graduate. You don't have to worry; we'll make sure they can stay."

"Well, call me when you know more."

ℙ

By this time, Mark was aware of the latest chapter in our family saga. Thanks to his strong determination to make a full recovery, his physical rehabilitation was going extremely well. Already he had moved from a wheelchair to a walker, and as his balance improved, he would soon trade the walker for a cane.

Mark agreed that if the boys were to come live with us, they would have to stay until they finished high school. As the days passed with no word from Lisa, I decided to give her a call. It was a Thursday night; it seemed we always talked on Thursdays.

"Hello, Lisa! What's up?"

"Deron and Jeff are back with Monica," she said.

"Wha-a-a-t?" I couldn't believe my ears.

"Yeah, Larry said he'd give her a job at his new and used clothes store."

"His what?" I tried to picture what Lisa was telling me.

"Larry and Kate are so proud of that store."

"Are they still dealing drugs?" I asked.

"How do you think they got the store?" Lisa said. "Although they are trying to stop."

"How?" I asked. I'd learned that when it came to drugs, trying to stop could mean practically anything or nothing at all.

"They take methadone," she replied.

"They take what?"

"Methadone. You know, the stuff people who use the needle take."

"How does it help them?" I asked.

"It curbs their desire to want to use."

I knew I had heard about methadone; I'd even seen people take it on television. But I didn't really know how it worked.

"Well, at least it's a step," I said. "I believe Larry really wants to stop, but he's just so addicted. All we can do is pray. But poor Jeff. It's bad enough seeing his mama on crack, and then the only person willing to keep him while she was in jail was an addict uncle! Boy, those kids have been through a lot!"

"Yeah, I know. They all need counseling!" She said it with a laugh. Unable to help myself, I found I was laughing too.

"I know, girl, you have to laugh to keep from crying. But what they really need is Jesus! Lisa, when you know Jesus, the only thing your body cries out for is His righteousness."

I had never before talked about spiritual things with Lisa. I don't know why. Maybe it's because she's older than I am, and I didn't want to seem disrespectful. Or perhaps it's because my family already treated me as if I thought I was better than they. Talking to them about living right might make them dislike me all the more, I thought.

But I did feel we needed to talk about it. Lisa acted as if she knew Jesus, but her life-style didn't always show it.

"Lisa, I don't know how Monica got so caught up in all that," I said. "It seems that once she made the mistake of playing a role in breaking up Donna and her husband, she couldn't get it together. It's been downhill ever since. Too bad we didn't have a daddy at home. It makes me upset just thinking about him and the kind of father he was."

"René, you can't hold on to being mad at Mr. Goree. You have to let that go."

"I have. I don't hold anything against him, but what upsets me is that he hasn't changed. He's been living the same old hustling life for more than 60 years! I understand that his mom died when he was a little boy, and because he was an only child, his daddy spoiled him. It taught him to be irresponsible. But you'd think after 10 kids he'd have learned some responsibility by now! Where is he, anyway?"

"Down at Miss Esther's."

"Right. That's where he's been since I can remember. Down at Miss Esther's. That's where he was when he had his first heart attack!" I said it with an attitude.

"René, I know. Girl, we didn't know what to do!"

"Remember, Lisa? We thought he was gone! He would have died doing just what he loved, being on the five points. You know they say home is where the heart is, and his heart is definitely on the five points. Well, at least I'm glad to hear that Monica will be working."

"She has to," said Lisa.

"Why doesn't she get a real job? Hanging out with Larry is not a good thing." I was getting depressed. "Lisa,

I'd better let you go."

"Before you do, are you and Mark still willing to keep the boys? Because these kids don't need to be around all this mess. We need to start thinking about them and let Monica do her own thing."

"Yes, we'll take them."

"OK I'll talk to you later."

𝓟

"Mark, if they come we will not allow my family to drive us crazy! And I'm not going to put a whole lot into them coming. We'll have to pray because they'll say one thing and do another. They want to help Deron and Jeff, but they also want Monica to get better overnight so they won't have to do something as drastic as take the boys away!"

Mark and I had waited several months, not sure whether the boys would be coming or not. In the middle of May, I received another call from Lisa.

"What's going on?" I asked.

"Jackie is on the other line," Lisa informed me. I could hear in her voice that my sister had just about had it.

"Hi, Jackie."

"Hey, girl," she replied.

"So, what's going on?" I asked again.

"We're calling Social Services on Monday," said Jackie. "Monica is too much."

"I thought you guys said she was doing better."

"René, we went over there, and there really ought to be a law against how she keeps that apartment," said Lisa. "She was so loaded it ain't even funny. Those kids don't deserve to live like that."

"You guys aren't saying anything we don't already know," I said. "All we ever do is talk."

"We know. But we're dead serious this time. Something has to be done. It's bad!"

I knew it had to be bad for them to say they were going to turn Monica in to Social Services.

"Will you guys be able to keep them so they can finish the school year?" I asked.

"Yeah. We just want to make sure you and Mark are still willing to keep them after that," said Lisa.

"We are," I said. "We're willing just as long as you guys know they have to stay with us until they're out of school."

"Cool. We'll call Social Rehabilitation Services (S.R.S.) on Monday. Monica won't send them to you willingly because without them, she can't get that monthly check. As sad as it sounds, that's the only reason she wants them," said Jackie.

"She loves them; she's just addicted. Call and let me know what S.R.S. says," I told them before saying goodbye.

ဗ

Mark was just pulling into the garage as I hung up

the phone. I didn't give him time to get inside the house.

"Mark, I think they're serious this time. I just got off the phone with Lisa and Jackie."

To tell you the truth, I was a little apprehensive about how Mark would take it. Although we had discussed the boys coming at some point in the future, it looked like the time was finally here.

"Monica must be driving them crazy," I continued. "I can tell by the tone of their voices that they're tired. I'm just tired of talking about it! If they're coming, I wish they'd just go ahead and get it all set up."

"You know your sisters, so we won't work on changing the room until they get here," Mark responded. Thinking another moment, he said, "You know, these are not the same little boys we had before. They're teenagers now. It's going to be like having two men living in our home."

"I know, Mark. But if it doesn't work, at least we'll have tried. And if they don't respect you, they'll just have to go back. It's as simple as that."

I said this knowing that it would be nearly impossible to send the boys away after they'd been here for any length of time, especially since they had nowhere else to go except foster care. I prayed that the Lord would work everything out. We knew they wouldn't be used to a lot of structure, including school, homework and other disciplines. But I truly believed that through prayer, God would take care of everything.

ℙ

Monday morning, I went to the office with a full agenda. But I couldn't concentrate. My eyes stayed fixed on the phone—and all I could think was, *Why in the world are they taking so long to call?* When the phone finally rang, I nearly jumped out of my skin.

"Hello," I said nervously. Thank heavens it was Lisa.

"Hey, René. I wanted to let you know that Jackie and I met with the caseworker today at Monica's, and girl, you can tell that Monica was waiting for the drug man. She kept looking out the window as if she was looking for somebody. That girl ain't got no sense."

I murmured my agreement, waiting for her to go on.

"Do you know that she had that no-good man there? The only thing he had to say was, 'Um, if you take the boys, does that mean Monica won't get any more benefits?' I guess they call welfare 'benefits' now. Like she was retiring from a job or something! The reality is, she's losing her job as a mother. Girl, I wanted to knock him out."

Lisa told me that during the entire meeting, Monica said almost nothing. All she seemed to care about was the monthly check.

"They kept telling Jackie and me that we were wrong for turning them in to the 'crackers,'" Lisa said. "She really needs help, but it's time to take care of the kids."

"I know, Lisa."

"When we went to get Deron, he was sitting on the fence behind the apartments. He didn't even care to tell his mama goodbye. He had some bad boy's cellular phone in his pocket. Girl, we really don't know about him, but we do know he doesn't need to be here."

"What about Jeff?" I asked.

"The social worker picked him up from school. She said he didn't say anything."

"How sad, Lisa. It's like they're yo-yos. Can you imagine being taken from your own mother? I don't care how tough times were for us; I would have died if someone had taken me away from Ma-Dear. I pray she gets herself together because I know her kids want to be with her. Monica's circumstances may seem bad to us, but it's what they're used to."

I was beginning to sound the way my sisters did when they talked us into sending the boys back the first time. But it was true. Children need their mothers. I wished I could tie Monica up until she got all the drugs out of her system, then wave a magic wand and change her into the mom the boys deserved.

This time I hung up the phone with a sense of relief. Finally, it was over. The boys were coming to live with us until they finished high school. At the age of 18, they could decide for themselves where to live and what to do with their lives.

𝔓

Unlike the first time they came, the boys were now old enough to travel alone.

"Mark, the bus gets in tonight around 11:00 p.m."

"Yes, René, I know. We'll leave around 10:00 p.m. so that when they get off the bus, we'll be right there."

Chapter 7
The Second Time Around

I really didn't know how or what to feel.

They won't be little boys any more, I reminded myself again and again. Every anxious thought opened another door—another "what if" for my mind to explore. Standing in the bus station as we watched each passenger come through the door, I whispered, "Lord, I am not going to worry about it; I know you'll handle everything."

"There they are, René!"

At first I saw only Jeff. The duffel bag he had slung over his shoulder held all of his possessions. I noticed he still wasn't wearing his glasses; he squinted as his eyes searched the station for us. But the look on his face said, *I've finally made it to safety.* Perhaps Jeff's relief wasn't about his coming to Kansas to live with us, but because he was under the wing of his big brother, his protector.

Deron was right behind him. He wore a pair of baggy white jeans that made it difficult for him to walk. Even his sneakers were too big. He scooted his way into the station.

Sizing the boys up in those first few moments, I saw that Deron was still the strong tower of the two. Life had thrown him a lot of blows. He was practically emotionless. Only his smile revealed his brokenness. I immediately felt in my spirit that Deron had arrived just in time. A person with any street smarts could tell he'd been involved with the wrong kind of people, probably a gang.

"Hi, Deron! Hi, Jeff! Give your Aunt René a hug."

They each gave me one of those pat-on-the-back kind of hugs. Both boys were as handsome as ever, and Lisa had made sure they had on clean clothes. Grinning shyly, they shook Mark's hand, but neither looked especially excited to see us.

"It's good to see you guys. Is this everything?" Mark motioned to the one box and duffel bag they had carried off the bus.

"Yeah, that's it," said Jeff.

"Well, let's go then. How was the bus ride?"

"It was OK. Jeff kept asking the driver if we were almost to Kansas."

"I was tired. That was a long ride."

As we drove home, the boys reacquainted themselves with Kansas City, remembering places they had seen before and trying to figure out the way to our house, which would soon become their new home.

"You guys know we moved, don't you? We don't live on 95th Street anymore."

"Yeah, Aunt Lisa told us."

"Actually, this house is a little bigger, and you guys will have your own bathroom. Remember last time? You had to share with me!"

They both chuckled. A minute later Mark said, "OK, we're here!"

The boys' eyes grew as big as saucers. They looked first at our new home and then at us, unable to conceal their astonishment.

"Who else lives with you guys?"

"Nobody, Deron. God must have known when He gave us this house that we'd need room for two young men."

I could tell by his expression that he didn't know what I meant. The crinkles in his nose gave him away. We got out of the car and went into the house.

"Are you guys hungry?"

"No. We ate a lot of stuff on the bus."

"Then I'll just show you your room, we'll call your Aunt Lisa, and since it's late, we'll get ready for bed. I don't know about you guys, but I'm tired. It's going on 2:00 a.m.!"

I could tell by the way they looked at me that this time of night was when things started hopping back in Denver. But they said nothing and began to get ready for bed. Just as when they were children, they were totally cooperative and compliant. I could tell they were still used to adapting, never having been given a choice or a voice in the matter.

"I'll make breakfast in the morning. You guys like waffles?"

"Yeah," they said in unison.

"Well, let's go to bed and we'll talk some more to-morrow."

Our house is equipped with a security alarm, mostly for my use when Mark is out of town. It's more of a psychological thing than anything else; I really do believe that the Lord protects me from all harm and danger. When it's my time to go, it will be my time.

But that night, we turned on the alarm. Not knowing what to expect, we figured that if Deron or Jeff tried to leave, we'd be awakened by the noise. The next morning Mark and I intended to cover the ground rules with the boys—something we hadn't done the first time they lived with us, although we really should have.

We all slept peacefully that night. I woke up the next morning with a sense of excitement that the boys had made it safely. Once again they would have a chance at a new life and freedom from the worries of the past.

φ

Sunlight streamed through the tall windows that stretched from one side of our kitchen to the other. The golden rays made the room so bright that there was no need for me to turn on the lights. Just the thought of cooking breakfast this morning gave me joy. I wanted the smell of bacon, eggs, hash-brown potatoes, and waffles to waft through the house and tease the boys awake. I wanted to give them a morning to remember.

I could only imagine what Deron and Jeff awoke to mornings in Denver. But this morning would be different. Jeff would know that he would always have food, and Deron would see that he no longer had to worry about how he would get meals for himself and his brother. I wanted them both to sense that Mark and I would now handle all of the adult responsibilities. They could take off their battle fatigues. The war was over!

"Breakfast will be ready in about 10 minutes," I shouted up the stairs.

When the boys appeared at the table, they were both in boxer shorts. Deron had his do-rag on.

Oh goodness. Mark is not going to go for this! I thought. *How long can I get away with saying they don't know any better?*

"Deron, did you and Jeff sleep all right?"

"Yeah."

The four of us made small talk as we ate our breakfast, mostly trying to break the ice. The boys probably had a lot of questions, but as usual they didn't ask. Eventually, Mark and I forged our way into more serious subjects, like the ground rules we hoped to establish.

"Listen, guys. Mark and I believe it's important that we talk about the ground rules. We know you're teenagers now, and a lot has changed since you were last here. First of all, do you know why you're here?"

Deron spoke up quickly and said, "Well, I thought we were coming to visit for a couple of weeks."

"Is that what somebody told you, Deron?" I asked.

"No. I just thought that. Nobody really told us anything."

No one told them what was happening? I shouldn't have been so surprised. Nobody ever cared to tell the boys anything; they just tossed them here and there, from person to person and place to place.

"Well, I should have figured that, Deron. That's why it's important for us to talk. Now, it's my understanding that the social worker and your aunts Lisa, Jackie and Donna made the decision to have you guys removed from your mom because the environment was too bad. Is that right?"

"Yeah."

"I guess."

"Jeff, how did you feel about your living situation?" I asked.

"I don't know. It was all right," he replied.

"Deron?"

"It was all right." He answered so quietly that I could barely hear him.

"I'll be honest. For your Aunt Lisa to do what she did, something had to be going on," I said. "The last thing anybody wants to do is to take you away from your own mother. I don't know what was going on because I wasn't there, but you boys need to know we've spent years running behind Monica, trying to get her to seek some professional help. Not for our benefit, but for herself and for you."

I paused a minute to let that sink in.

"You guys are getting older," I continued, "and it's time someone paid attention to your needs. Your mom did the best she could, but it's hard when you have an addiction. I'm sorry if nobody told you the truth. Mark and I will be as open and honest as possible."

The boys sat in silence. Deron did not look happy.

He looked as if someone had tricked him into coming to Kansas. I hated to say anything more, but he needed to know the truth.

"As far as I know, you will not be able to return to your mom until she gets herself together." I felt as if I'd dropped a bomb. "Maybe by your coming here, she'll be motivated to get some help. Until she does, I've agreed to keep you until you turn 18. Then you'll be out of school and ready to start your own lives. We know it's been several years since we all lived together, but if we want to make this thing work, it's important that we communicate. Now, I've said a lot. How do you guys feel?"

They didn't have anything to say—just "OK." What else could they say? If they chose not to stay with us, they'd end up in a boys' shelter or foster care. Even if that was acceptable to them, it certainly wasn't to me!

"Our goal is to help you graduate from high school and become respectable men," I said. "We haven't given up on your mom, but now that you guys are getting older, it's time to focus on what you want out of life."

I wrapped up the ground rules with, "Mi casa es su casa. You got that, buddy?" They chuckled a little, and I explained that we wanted them to think of our house as their own. Then it was time to make a plan for the day.

"When we're finished eating, Mark will take you to get a haircut. Remember Ralph?"

"Yes."

"Good. That's who will be cutting your hair. Next week I'll spend some time trying to get you guys involved in some daytime activities, so you'll have something to do while Mark and I are at work. I'd hate for you to be cooped up in the house all day."

They boys studied me warily, as if to say, *Well, here she goes! Now she's gonna take over our lives.* I felt bad because I wasn't offering them a choice. Given the option, I was afraid they might choose to do nothing all day.

"Deron, I was thinking about letting you get a job. What do you think?"

"That's fine with me."

"Have you ever worked before?"

"We used to sell candy, and I used to baby-sit."

"What did you do with your money?"

"Mostly just bought us something to eat."

"Well, thank God you had enough sense to work so you could eat. Now let's talk about church. You guys know we go to church every Sunday."

They nodded in agreement. "We used to go to church with Luther sometimes," Jeff said.

"I'm glad to hear that, Jeff. You know, God has been too good for us not to give Him some time out of our week. Now, Mark still directs the youth choir and teaches Sunday school. I'm an usher. I think it would be great for you guys to become active too. It'll give you a chance to meet other kids your age, and you won't have to sit every Sunday without participating in the Lord's work. I know you said you used to go to church, but do you guys believe in Jesus?"

They looked at me as if they thought I was crazy.

"Yeah, we do."

"Good. I want you to know that just because your mom and Luther do drugs, that doesn't mean God doesn't love them. God loves everybody. What He doesn't like is bad actions like doing drugs. And what He wants people to realize is that they don't need drugs to feel good or to get away from their problems, because guess what?"

They both just looked at me.

"When they come down from the high, nothing has changed. As a matter of fact, their problems just get worse. I truly believe that life is about decisions—choices that are based on the realities of right and wrong. God even gives us a choice whether to love Him or something or someone instead of Him. If we choose the world and the things in it over Him, then when we die, we've chosen to burn in hell."

There was a long silence, and I figured they'd had enough of a sermon for one morning.

"Anybody want more waffles?" I asked. They all just looked at me, including Mark. "Good," I said. "That means everybody must be full! By the way, do either of you boys know how to cook?"

Jeff piped up, "Yeah, I can!"

"I'm glad because I don't want to be the only one cooking for this crew," I said, only half joking. "Deron, we'll have to teach you."

Deron smirked and said, "Cooking is for girls."

"That's not true. Is Jeff a girl?"

"No."

"Are all the great chefs female?"

"I don't know."

"The answer is no. Who would cook for you if you lived by yourself?"

"I'd probably just eat out."

"Oh, so you want to spend all your money on food!"

Deron smiled as he gave thought to my question. As I straightened up the kitchen, we discussed the economics of buying groceries as opposed to eating out every night.

"Do you have anything to wear to church tomorrow?" I asked the boys as I gave the countertop a final scrub.

"No, not really," Jeff said softly. Then he remembered, "Deron has a suit, and we did bring our Sunday shoes."

"Good. Let me take a look at what you have, and we'll make a trip to the mall for the rest." Folding my dishcloth, I turned and faced the boys. "Guys, all I'm going to ask you to do is to make sure you keep your room cleaned and your clothes washed, take out the trash, and a few other things we'll think of as we go along. What's most important is that we communicate and pray as a family. Also, this is your home now, so treat it as your own."

ꝑ

It seemed as if we'd just finished breakfast when the brightness of day became the dusk of the evening. By the time we finished our shopping, the day was gone. Mark and I were exhausted.

"Let's pray tonight," we told the boys. "We'll come to your room in about 20 minutes." As Mark and I waited for the boys to get ready for bed, we quietly discussed how we must have been throwing off their entire schedule. Church and school had never been a reason for Deron and Jeff to get to bed. They probably went to bed wherever they fell asleep, without ever wondering what time it was.

Our prayer time that night was an experience I'll never forget. I knew in my heart that Deron and Jeff were prime targets for Satan. The life-style they had been exposed to had left the door wide open for demonic activity and oppression.

"Why don't we all pray—Deron, Jeff, me and then Mark," I said. "Just say what you feel. Talk to God like you mean it; tell Him what's on your heart." I didn't know if what I said made sense to them, but I hoped they'd eventually understand that only God could truly help them solve all of their problems. I wanted them to know how vital it was to go to God for everything, little or big.

As we knelt around the bed, Deron prayed, "Dear God, I want to thank You for a beautiful morning. Dear Lord, thank You for letting my brother and me make it to Kansas safe. Please watch over mom, Luther and the Goree and Parson families. Amen."

Then Jeff began, "Dear God, thank You for the beautiful morning..." When he ran out of words, Jeff repeated what his brother had said, finishing with a prayer for his mom and Luther.

Next it was my turn. But as I began to pray, all of the lights in the house went out, an eerie feeling enveloped the room. You could actually feel the darkness, as if it were a presence. I continued to pray—not casually, but with the power of the Holy Spirit—calling on Jesus to remove anything from our home that was not of Him, and rebuking evil spirits in the name of Jesus as the tears rolled down my face.

It was only after a few minutes of intense prayer that all of a sudden, the lights came back on. Mark and I thanked God mightily. We didn't know what had happened, but we knew that something was not right. We asked the boys if they were O.K.

"Yeah," they both replied. Jeff wanted to know what had happened.

"I don't know. But don't worry, because whatever it is or was, it can't touch us because God protects us. Now you guys go ahead and go to bed."

We told them we loved them and walked down the hall to our room as if we were brave warriors. As soon as we closed our door, we looked at each other in amazement. We could only conclude that Satan was mad because he no longer had a hold on those boys. They would now have a chance to know Jesus and live fruitful lives. It was clear that evil had come into our home. Whether or not it was gone, we did not know. We only knew that we had to pray without ceasing.

Chapter 8
Summertime in a New City

"Deron and Jeff, I've enrolled you both in the Boys' and Girls' Club. It'll give you something constructive to do besides sit around the house all day. And Deron, we need to start looking for a summer job for you."

He smiled. "I'll have to get it OK'd by Social Services first."

It occurred to me that I was beginning to plan the boys' lives—something I hadn't intended to do. But it happened almost automatically, as if by default. The boys never seemed to know what they wanted to do. I suspect that throughout their lives they had simply done what others told them to do, whether right or wrong. As a result, they never seemed to know their own minds. Rarely did they express their desires—what they wanted to do or to eat.

It came naturally for me to jump in and make plans for them, often telling them what kinds of activities they wanted to get involved in or what foods they liked to eat. *How long will this go on before they speak up and make their own choices?* I wondered. Until then, I would do what I had to do. I became a woman with a plan!

In an effort to get to know the boys better and open the lines of communication, I often asked bold questions.

"Have either of you two ever done drugs?"

"No, but Luther used to make us drink," said Deron.

"That's because he doesn't know any better," I told

him. "No child has any business drinking. Life is about choices, and you should never be forced to do anything like drinking, whether you're a child or an adult. I chose not to drink."

Deron wanted to know why.

"Let's think about it," I said. "What have alcohol and drugs ever done for our family? What I saw going on when I was growing up and even what's happening today—none of it is positive!"

Deron was skeptical. "You mean you don't drink *anything?"* he asked.

"Nothing, Deron."

"Not even wine? Wine is OK, isn't it?"

"Not for me because it's like fire, and I choose not to play with fire. You like playing with fire?" He shrugged his shoulders. "I've tasted champagne, and I work with people who consume alcohol. Does it make me better than they are? No."

"Does the Bible say you can't drink?" Deron asked.

"No. But it does say that a drunkard won't inherit the kingdom of God." I was referring to 1 Corinthians 6:10. "Deron, I have never been able to figure out why a person has to drink. Why fill your system with something that could make you act uncontrollable and out of this world? Thank you, but I'll pass. Now, I would like to get drunk in the Holy Spirit!"

"How do you do that?"

"That's when God's Spirit consumes your body with

overwhelming joy, and you're so happy that you find yourself in a state of uncontrollable excitement. The difference is, you wake up the next morning feeling better than you did before, unlike being drunk from alcohol, which makes you wake up the next day with a hangover!"

Deron laughed and nodded his head. I could tell he didn't know what to make of me.

"So, Deron, I take it that you like to drink."

"Well, I don't see anything wrong with it sometimes."

Not surprised by his answer, I asked him, "Deron, why are you here?"

"I don't know."

"You're here because of drugs and drinking! If it weren't for those two things, you'd probably still be in Denver with your mother. It's because she chooses to use that she can't take care of her kids. That's why it's not cool or OK with me, some of the time or anytime! It destroyed your mother."

I hoped and prayed that the seeds I was planting would fall on fertile ground.

𝛗

As we had planned, Deron and Jeff attended their first day at the Boys' and Girls' Club summer camp. Wondering how they had adjusted, I couldn't wait to pick them up afterward.

"So, how'd it go?" I asked as they hopped in the car.

"All right. There are a lot of kids there," said Deron.

"I know. Since you're part of the older group, maybe next year you can be one of the counselors," I said to Deron.

"Yeah, I'd like that."

"Both of you can be good role models for the younger kids. Hopefully one day you'll be able to give back. You know, God can work anywhere, but I think He sent you back to Kansas to give you an opportunity that will affect the rest of your lives! If you're obedient to Him, you'll be successful," I said, ignoring the dubious looks on their faces. The boys always shook their heads in disagreement whenever I told them they were intelligent or handsome.

I glanced at Jeff in the rearview mirror. He had been quiet since he'd climbed in the car.

"Jeff, what do you want to be when you grow up?"

"A basketball player."

"You know what? You can be a basketball player," I said. "What do you think it takes to be a basketball player?"

"Practice!" he replied.

"Right. What else?"

"I don't know." He seemed puzzled.

"Perseverance, tenacity and commitment among other things. Most of all, you've got to want to do it!"

Jeff looked at me with uncertainty, as if he couldn't believe I was actually telling him that he could become a professional basketball player.

"Deron, what do you want to be?"

"A rapper."

"Who's your favorite rapper?" I asked. I already knew the answer, but I wanted to hear him confirm it.

"Tupac."

Just hearing him say the name made my flesh crawl. This was someone whom I did not consider a good role model.

"Why Tupac?" I did my best to conceal my disapproval.

"Because I can relate to him."

"Relate to him!" *So much for hiding my emotion.* "What do you mean?"

Deron gave a little smile and said he didn't know. Sensing that he'd picked up on my disappointment, I changed my tone.

"So if you want to be a rapper, and I'm Puffy Combs..."

They looked at each other with a funny expression. *How does she know him?*

"Um-hum," I went on, "you didn't know I knew who Puff Daddy was, did you?"

They both laughed.

"OK, Deron, I'm Puff Daddy. You want to be a rapper, so what would you do or say to me?"

"I don't know," he replied. He was still laughing at the idea of me as Puffy Combs.

"What do you mean, you don't know? Why are you laughing? Is that how you'd act? Oh, so you didn't think

I knew anything about rapping. Yeah, I know you think because I live out here and I love Jesus that I don't know what goes on. Don't forget that I come from the same place you do! I chose not to do some things, but I've seen a whole lot. Now stop laughing and let me hear you rap!"

"I used to write in Denver," Deron said.

"Good. I'll get you a tablet, and you can start writing. These days rappers are a dime a dozen, and you're telling me this is what you want to do. If so, we need to make sure you're ready!"

ꝓ

A few days later, the subject of the boys' future came up again.

"I don't know much about basketball or rapping," I said, "but I'll support you on one condition."

"What's that?" Deron asked.

"That you both graduate from high school. I don't expect you to make straight A's, but I do expect you to pass all your classes. Did you both go to school every day in Denver?"

"No," they answered.

"Why not?"

"Sometimes our lights were out and we didn't know what time it was—or Mom just didn't wake us up," said Jeff.

"What kind of grades did you make?"

"They were OK."

"How about you, Deron?"

"I don't know."

"You don't know?" I didn't give him time to answer. As far as we were now concerned, what had happened in Denver was ancient history. "Oh well, that's what you did then," I said. "The question is, what do you want to do now?"

I was getting used to the long silences that always seemed to follow my questions. Deron had been hanging on my every word, but he seemed unsure how to answer.

"Deron, you have a choice. At your age, you can work at a fast-food restaurant, the grocery store or Dairy Queen. Which do you choose?"

"The grocery store."

"All right! I'll call Schnuck's right now. It's within walking distance, so let's see if you can meet with the manager. I can help you get this first job, but you'll need to learn these things for yourself before long." He nodded in agreement. "We'll do a little role playing before we go in to see the manager."

❦

The day of Deron's interview, I left work early. The manager asked us to come at 4p.m., but I insisted that Deron be ready by 3:30. "It's important to arrive early because you always want to make a good impression," I told him.

I'll bet I'm more nervous than Deron is. Lord, please make it all work out, I prayed as I pulled into our driveway.

Deron came to the car looking so handsome and nice. "Are you scared?" I asked.

"No."

At least that makes one of us, I thought.

"Well, you don't have to be scared," I reminded us both. "Don't forget, you can do all things through Christ, who strengthens you. And it won't hurt to remember all the things I've told you." In the last few days, I had given Deron a crash course on how to behave in a job interview. How I hoped he'd remember the basics: *Look the manager in the eye, give a firm handshake, and by all means, speak clearly.*

We were about five minutes away from the store when I could sense something different in Deron. Without any indication why, he began to open up and share his feelings.

"I remember when I was in Denver, I did a lot of bad things," he said.

"Bad things like what?"

"I used to push people a lot."

"Why?"

"I don't know. It made me feel good," he said.

"It made you feel good to push people around?"

"Yeah!"

"I call people like that bullies."

"I know, but something in me made me do it."

"Were you mad?"

"No. It just made me feel good. I used to laugh at old people a lot too."

"Well, Deron, if you keep on living, one day you'll be old too."

Maybe talking eased his nerves. I was thankful he was beginning to feel comfortable enough to share his inner thoughts with me.

"It's real quiet around here," he said.

"You think so?"

"Yeah. At home you hear police cars all day long. Kids are in the streets, and people are fighting and everything."

No matter what the boys told me, I always made it a point to keep my composure. It made me appear strong to them, while inside, a torrent of tears was on the verge of pouring out.

"Well, Deron, that's because people choose how they want to live. Just because you live in the 'hood doesn't mean that you have to act bad. I've learned that home is truly where the heart is. I didn't grow up around peace and quiet—as a matter of fact, it was chaos. But you think folks out here don't argue, fuss and fight?"

He shrugged. I'm not sure he thought it possible that they did.

"Well, they do. They just choose not to do it in the streets."

"It seems like everywhere I go, somebody gets hurt," he said.

"What do you mean?"

"I don't know. It just seems like somebody always gets hurt."

"If you weren't the cause of the pain, then how do you figure it's your fault?"

"I don't know."

"I'm going to choose to believe that bad things don't happen just because you're there. You are a nice, respectable young man with a big future ahead of you. That is, if you choose to live right."

What is it he's trying to tell me? I wondered. There was obviously some pain he was trying to uncover, but I lacked the insight to help him. I hoped he felt some relief in having shared his heart.

ℙ

"We're here," I said as we parked near the grocery store. "Don't be nervous." *That was probably the wrong thing to say!* "Now, hold your head up high. You've got nothing to be ashamed of."

My plan was that Deron would answer all of the manager's questions. But in my overprotective zeal, I wound up doing most of the talking. Fortunately, he got the job.

"I knew you could do it!" I said on the way home. Deron was all smiles. "You should be so proud of yourself. You just got your first job! I'll teach you how to manage your money. But the first thing we need to do is thank Jesus."

"I know. I already did that," he said.

"Good!"

"I never had a real job before."

"I'll have to take you and Jeff both to get I.D. cards and wallets—and we'll open you a bank account too." I was rambling in my excitement, but he was right with me, nodding in agreement. I don't know who was more excited.

𝓟

When he started his new job, I asked that Deron begin tithing 10 percent of his income.

"This is your opportunity to show an expression of thanks to the Lord," I said. "It's what we're asked to give as Christians."

Deron had no problem with tithing. His problem, most likely, was figuring out the 10 percent. Math was not Deron's favorite subject. But when it came to my advising him about his money, he was always receptive. This didn't surprise me since the boys typically did what others told them to do.

"You can keep the job during the school year, but if it's too much and your grades aren't where they should be, I'll have to ask you to quit."

Again, he nodded in agreement. I never gave Deron an opportunity to say what he wanted to do with his money. My obsession to see him achieve and beat all the odds outweighed my desire to see him learn from his own decisions. Praying that he would understand why I did the

101

things I did, I also hoped he and Jeff would know that I wouldn't make such decisions if I didn't truly love them.

Deron worked all that summer. He even won a certificate for being the employee of the week. Without hesitation, he did exactly what I asked him to do with every paycheck. He was so proud just to have money in his pocket—money he had actually earned; money he didn't have to buy food with or give away to help someone feed a drug habit.

Mark and I were proud of Deron too. He had an infectious smile and a heart bigger than Kansas. The poor boy had been through so much; it was a wonder he was functioning so well. Jeff, too, seemed very comfortable with his new life-style. He looked as if the weight of the world had been lifted off his shoulders.

P

Summer seemed to end quickly, and soon school was on the horizon. What a change it was going to be for Deron and Jeff to go from a predominantly black school to a mostly white school! *Thank God they know how to adapt,* I thought for at least the hundredth time.

Jeff would be going to the local middle school. Deron would attend a nearby high school that the local community thought could do no wrong. It was hard for me to picture them attending schools so opposite of what they had known in Denver. I didn't want them to be treated any differently from the other kids. Black kids would be few in number, and I figured these kids probably didn't come from an environment anything like what Deron and

Jeff had experienced.

I remember sitting in the counselor's office as we enrolled Deron in high school and having to pray silently to keep from giving the counselor a piece of my mind and walking out the door.

"Deron, there is a drastic difference between this school and the one you attended in Colorado," he said smugly. "You were one of the majority there. Here you will be in the minority."

So what! I said to myself as my mind began to race. I didn't want this man talking to Deron at all. I had already told him everything he needed to know about school!

"What was it like in Denver?" the counselor asked.

"What do you mean?" asked Deron.

"Was there a lot of fighting?"

What kind of questioning is this? I wanted to know. *Is he trying to find out if Deron is violent?*

"Yeah, there was fighting," Deron answered.

"Were there gangs?"

"Yes."

"Did you belong to any?"

"No. But I knew some people in gangs."

If I had known then what I know now, I'd have told that counselor that the schools in Colorado have gangs just like the gangs at his school—the ones we never heard about before Deron enrolled there. I didn't want to hear another word about how superior this school was compared to the mostly black school Deron had gone to in Denver. The nerve of him!

"If I may, let me interrupt to say that I'm Deron's aunt, and my husband and I have kept him before here in Kansas. He and his brother spent a couple of years in the Shawnee Mission school district and got along fine with everyone. While I know that his school in Colorado had a much higher percentage of blacks, attending this school will not be a problem for Deron."

So let's move on to another subject, I wanted to say. This man was getting on my nerves, but I was trying to act like a Christian woman with some sense.

"I would really like to hear Deron speak," he said.

"I know you would," I replied with a forced smile, "but I'm speaking for him today. Deron's been through a lot, and now he has a chance to move forward. As you can see from his transcript, he didn't attend school very much last year. Our goal is to get him into the right classes so he can graduate." *Not sit here and talk about how much better this school is than his school in Colorado,* I wanted to add. Deron looked relieved that the talk had shifted away from his past.

The counselor told us that Deron did not have enough credits to be classified as a sophomore, but that with hard work, he might be able to graduate on time. As we left his office, he told Deron that he was lucky to have an aunt like me.

I don't believe in luck. I think God knew what Deron needed before time even began. I didn't know if that counselor had a method to his madness, but I asked the Lord to forgive me if my behavior toward him was wrong.

On the way home, I asked Deron what he thought about the fact that he would be classified as a freshman and not a sophomore. I could tell he was feeling embarrassed, and in my opinion, sometimes the only way to get beyond shame is to talk about it.

"There's no reason to be ashamed," I told him. "You're really blessed that you get this chance to make a new start in life. Nobody here knows you, and you have a great opportunity to make a good first impression by doing things right."

A relieved smile came over Deron's face. I could tell the idea of a fresh start appealed to him.

"So hold your head up and do what you have to do to graduate," I said. "I don't expect you to make all A's, B's or C's, but I want you to pass." I believed Deron had the ability to graduate with honors if he put his mind to it.

ꝑ

For the next few months, Deron and I spent every night from 6:30 to 10:00, midnight or even later, working to get him caught up. I had no idea they could give a child so much homework! There were assignments for every class. My only consolation was that I knew good and well that other parents had to be up late with their kids as well—perhaps doing the work for them!

Deron was very patient, but all the work was taking a toll on both of us. Fortunately, Deron liked a few of his classes, especially drama. In fact, his drama and math teachers were terrific and very understanding. They were his favorites.

It concerned me that when Deron started school, he acted as if he wanted nothing to do with the other kids. He wasn't interested in making friends, I believe because he secretly felt that they were too good for him. Deron probably thought that the other kids didn't have any problems—that they all had both parents at home, or that they knew nothing about dads who disappeared, drugs, alcohol and all the other things he had experienced. In Deron's eyes, these kids all had cars, money, intelligence and a spotless past.

To complicate matters, in the last five years all Deron had heard about white people was that they kept the black man down. Therefore, the thinking went, black folks had to "get our own." This was the stuff his mother's boyfriend used to feed him and Jeff—and it was hard for Deron to forget this way of thinking. He often talked about never wanting to forget his past. I could see that my lifestyle was a threat to him.

"Deron, life's about choices," I'd often say. "All people have problems, no matter what color they are. Problems don't discriminate. Believe me, I definitely haven't forgotten my past. It's what keeps me moving in a different direction! I could be doing drugs, stealing, killing or whatever. I chose not to live that type of life. If I teach you one thing, I want it to be that through Christ you can do anything."

I couldn't read Deron's mind, but I'd bet anything he was thinking, *Oh, no. Here she goes again!* Yet I felt it was my duty to teach him the right things in life. And at the front, back and center of all my teaching, I wanted

Deron to know who would help him through life's trials. That was Jesus Christ.

"Where people fall short is when they try to do it all by themselves, thinking they don't need any help at all," I told him. "What we've found in our family is that we try to live by gambling, selling drugs or doing anything just to make it. Who wants to worry about where the next dollar is coming from? I like my money guaranteed. That's why I work."

Chapter 9
Brother to Brother

We were grateful that things were going well; the boys were adjusting to us, and we felt good about having them here. Unfortunately, as fate would have it, our first major battle was about to begin.

Nick, a friend from church, picked up the boys from time to time, just to grab a bite to eat and talk. I never considered the possibility that Deron and Jeff would abuse the friendship of someone who was extending such generosity to them. I found out differently through a casual phone call.

"Hello?" I answered. It was Nick. The purpose of his call was to catch me up on the boys' last visit with him. But before the call ended, Nick happened to mention that he was missing a ring. I almost ignored the comment, but something finally registered.

"Did you say you're missing a ring?" I asked.

"Yeah," he told me.

I asked whether Nick thought the boys had something to do with the missing ring. He said he didn't think so, and our conversation ended. But as I hung up the phone, thoughts of doubt and disbelief filled my mind. I didn't want Nick to know what I was thinking, but I absolutely had to tell Mark.

℘

"Mark! I just finished talking to Nick, and he told me that one of his rings is missing. He didn't accuse Deron or Jeff, but it sounds like one of them may have stolen it. They were the only ones there when it turned up missing!"

"Well, René, what do you want to do?"

"I don't know, but when they get in from playing basketball, let's ask them."

Why would they do something like this? I wondered. *What would they do with Nick's ring? Does this mean they'll be stealing all the time? When we ask them about it, what if they say yes? Do we send them back home? Maybe they took it because they think they're going back to Denver anyway. I mean, what would they do with a ring besides wear it or sell it for some quick cash?*

Whatever the reason, I couldn't tolerate such behavior. As soon as the boys came home, we gathered in the family room and I took the bull by the horns.

"Deron, Jeff, we need to have a family meeting."

I could tell they wondered what was going on.

"When you guys first came here, we said that in order for us to get along, we would have to have open communication." They nodded in agreement. "Well, we have something to ask you, and it's important that you're up front and honest with us." I took a deep breath and went on.

"Nick called me today and said that he's missing one of his rings. He didn't accuse either of you, but I'm asking, did one of you take it?"

Both boys quickly denied it. I said I was glad to know that they wouldn't take something from someone who had been nothing but nice to them, and I dropped the issue. But later that night, I told Mark that I didn't know if I believed the boys. I did know that sooner or later, the Holy Spirit would reveal what had happened. As my mother always said, "Whatever you do in the dark will soon come to light." And that's exactly what happened.

Later that week while lying in bed, I heard the Holy Spirit say, *Get up and look under their dresser.* Immediately I popped up out of bed, moving so fast that even Mark didn't know where I was going. In the corner under the dresser, I found a man's ring.

My heart dropped to the floor. Even though I'd had my doubts about the boys, I wanted to believe that they wouldn't steal. Most of all, I wanted to trust them. Now I would have to call Nick and tell him that one of my nephews stole his ring. I didn't have a problem with calling personally, but it would be embarrassing for the boys to face the person who had been so nice to them, knowing how they had chosen to repay his kindness.

℘

When we confronted them with the evidence, Deron took it personally.

"I knew you guys would blame us if something like this ever happened."

"Deron, nobody is blaming you if you didn't take it. I'm asking you a simple question. Which one of you took the ring?"

"It don't matter. You wouldn't believe us," he said angrily.

"I wouldn't ask you the question if I wouldn't believe you."

Deron continued with his defensive remarks.

"I think maybe you've said enough, young man," I responded. "Maybe you should just be quiet."

But he wouldn't be quiet. Mark tried to intervene by asking him to show some respect. But Deron kept mouthing off for no apparent reason. I couldn't believe he had the gall to say he knew that we would blame them—especially since I had the evidence in my hand! Before I knew it, I was in Deron's face, asking him where he got the kind of nerve to talk like that. It was as if he had no fear, but neither did I! I even dared him to hit me. No matter what we said, he continued to defy us. Jeff never said a word.

"Get out now!" I finally yelled.

I knew Deron had nowhere to go, but at that moment I didn't care. I couldn't believe that a disturbance of this magnitude was taking place in my home. I knew that God could not have been pleased.

In the middle of it all, I called Nick and told him what had happened. He came right over and took both boys outside to give us all a chance to cool off. In the meantime, I called Lisa and told her the story. She told me I should just send the boys back.

"Back where? Colorado?" I asked. There, they'd be put in a foster home. I couldn't stand to think about that. But I was torn. No one had ever really cared for Deron and Jeff. Did they take the ring thinking that if they made us angry enough, we'd send them back to their carefree life-style? I didn't know what to do, but I wasn't ready to give up. I thought of how Christ had never given up on me—how He graciously gives me chance after chance.

After the episode with Deron, I felt that we all needed some space from one another. I arranged for Deron to stay with my nephew Brian, a nice young man with a level head, who was attending college in the city. Even after his brother was gone, Jeff didn't say a word.

My husband was convinced that the boys should return to Denver and was somewhat disappointed when I told him I wanted to give them another chance. I couldn't blame Mark. His house had been turned upside down by two difficult teenagers.

Deron stayed with Brian for a couple of days. Mark and I agreed that he could not return without apologizing for his attitude. Jeff kept his silence; in fact, he wouldn't even look at me.

A weekend passed, and Brian called to inform us that he'd be bringing Deron home late Sunday evening. As Mark and I discussed how to handle his return, we remarked that in all that had happened, we had never determined who had actually taken the ring.

"Mark, who do you think took it?" I asked.

"I don't know, René."

"I don't either," I said, "but I figure it was Jeff. He's so used to his brother taking care of him that he let Deron take the entire blame. Have you noticed he's never said a single word? It's probably best. I don't have the energy to listen to any more lies."

𝓟

Brian brought Deron home. We sat around the kitchen table and listened to a rehearsed apology. Deron never said he took the ring, but he said he was willing to take the blame. This confirmed my belief that Jeff had taken it. *Whoever took it, I'll probably never know,* I thought, *but at least it isn't my conscience that has to live with it.* These boys were like glue. They'd stick together no matter what. I told Mark that all we had to do was wait; the truth would win out in the end.

That night before bed, we had Bible study. Mark and I used the opportunity to talk about right and wrong choices and to explain about heaven and hell. These kids had no fear. They needed to understand the road where bad choices in life would lead them. In this world, that might mean jail or an early grave. After that, eternal damnation might await them.

Jeff had a lot of questions, but nothing we said seemed to bother Deron at all. This boy had been so brainwashed; wrong was right—as long as you didn't get caught! It would take a miracle to change his mind.

As we continued our discussion of what it meant to burn in hell, Jeff spoke up. "I have a confession to make," he said. Silence filled the room as he burst into tears.

"I-I-I-I took N-N-Nick's ring." The tears rolled down his face and fogged his glasses.

"Jeff, it's OK," I said. "I just want to thank you for telling the truth."

Rather than punishing Jeff, we embraced him for his breakthrough of honesty. We made sure he knew that

God forgives us for our sins, but that sometimes we still have to suffer the consequences. Although we too forgave him, he still had to apologize to Nick for stealing. I also felt that he owed Deron an apology.

In the midst of the tension, we broke into laughter when Deron released his frustration with Jeff.

"Man, why did you put us through so much confusion?"

Deron was willing to lie for his brother—that much was clear. He was Jeff's protector, and he cared for him like a son.

Chapter 10
Drama and Drama

Deron had to quit his job when school started. He didn't want to. It was his first job, and he liked it. I too was pleased that Deron enjoyed working but had to remind him of our agreement; it was more important that he pass his classes than have a job at this point in life. I hoped he would always want to work as a means of making a living; his background had taught him that there's always another way to make money.

Deron's drama class gave him an opportunity to come out of his shell—way out. Through drama, he met a few friends he could relate to. Unfortunately, it was obvious to Mark and me that these were not the kind of kids who were thinking about their future or Deron's.

Deron's behavior changed overnight. I noticed it one day when he seemed more talkative than usual. In fact, his whole demeanor was different. He was very bold—not afraid to say what was on his mind. *This is great if it means he's beginning to feel comfortable around Mark and me,* I thought. But as I watched him closely, I began to have a feeling something else was going on. *God forbid if he can only be this confident when he's high!*

At first I said nothing about it. But after several days of Deron's unusual behavior, I had to mention it to Mark.

"You know, René, I thought it was me," he said. "I didn't say anything to you because I wasn't sure, but I believe Deron is getting high."

"Oh my God in heaven!" It was as if I'd been punched in the stomach. I despised drugs because they had destroyed so many of the people I loved. Never in a million years did I think that drug use would occur in my own home. *What drugs could he be using?* I wondered. Before long, I would have my answer.

$\wp$

One day Deron was late coming home from school. He never ran late, so I asked him where he had been.

"I stayed after school for my drama class," he said nonchalantly.

"How did you get home?"

"I walked."

"Where's your rehearsal schedule?" I asked.

"I left it at school."

"Mm-hum."

Later in the week, I noticed that Deron was eating a lot. This was unusual for him. He wasn't a big eater; in fact, I often had to make him eat. *He's got the munchies,* I thought as I watched him devour a bag of chips. I had learned that word from my older brothers, who once explained to me what happens when people smoke weed. Marijuana makes you hungry, they told me.

Hoping to catch him off guard, I asked Deron, "Have you been smoking weed?"

"No," he said. I could tell my question had taken him by surprise.

"I'm going to take your word for it," I told him, "but

I want you to know that your red eyes and all this eating tell me something different than what you're saying. Don't forget, I knew about getting high before you were born."

I paused to give him a chance to respond. *I hope he realizes I'm not so naïve,* I said to myself. *If the boys think I'm a pushover, they'll try to get away with murder.*

"I know you think I'm square," I continued, "but there isn't much I don't know about. The things teens do today may go by different names or a new kind of slang, but it's no different than when I was growing up or what your mom and others in our family have done. Now, I think you need to take a shower because if you haven't been smoking weed, you certainly smell like it."

Deron could not say one word. He looked at me with his eyes wide open in amazement.

The nerve of him, I thought, *thinking he could out-smart me!* I had no idea how long he'd been getting high, but one thing I had told Deron and Jeff many times: the Lord would not allow wrongdoing to go on without my finding out about it.

Sometimes I believe that the most difficult position in the world is serving as a relative foster parent. You experience such a strange mix of emotions. When the child challenges your authority or acts destructively or defiantly, your first temptation is to send him somewhere else. *He's not my child, not my responsibility,* you think. But if you have any heart at all, you can't just return them to an agency as if they were actual foster kids. I believe the bond is significantly different.

Deron and Jeff were like my little brothers. Although

the thought crossed my mind, I couldn't come to grips with letting them go. I still believed that their being here was the will of God, and I wanted to do His will.

ቀ

That confrontation with Deron was the beginning of a nightmare. In the months to come, this teenager would practically drive us crazy.

It had been a few weeks since I had called the school to get an update on Deron's grades. Normally, I would leave a message for each of his teachers at least once a week. My motive was to check on his status regarding a possible graduation.

This time his drama teacher didn't have good news.

"Deron hasn't been staying after school for rehearsal," he said.

I asked to meet with the teacher, who showed me the practice schedule and the number of days Deron had missed. *Lord, here I am killing myself to make sure this boy gets all of his work done—and it's as if he doesn't even care!* I said to myself.

On the way home from the meeting, all I could think about was why Deron was refusing to make the right choices. I was doing all I knew to do. He had seen life at both ends of the spectrum. On the one end, he hadn't known where his next meal would come from. On the other, he didn't have to worry about such things. All he had to do was concentrate on school—and he couldn't even seem to do that!

"Oh, Mark! Deron has been lying," I told my husband that afternoon. "He's not turning in his work, and he's not going to school. Dear God in heaven, what are we going to do?"

"Where could he be if he's not in class?" Mark asked.

"I don't know. His teacher said a lot of the kids go over to Taco Hut."

At dinner that evening, I questioned Deron regarding his whereabouts.

"Help me out, buddy," I said. "I met with your drama teacher, and he told me you haven't been staying after school for practice or turning in your assignments. What's going on?"

"I don't know what he's talking about."

"What do you mean? This is your favorite class— the class you wanted to take. Where are you going if you're not staying for practice?"

"I don't know what he's talking about," Deron said defensively. "I do stay after school."

"OK, Deron. I'll try to believe you, but I can't think of any reason why a teacher would lie about you. Now, you know the school play is coming up, and the other students are counting on you. Mark my word, if you're not practicing, we'll surely find out."

Deron looked down at his plate, avoiding my eyes.

"It sounds like you've found some friends now," I said. "I thought you didn't want to be friends with none of those white people. Changed your mind when you found out people are people and it doesn't matter what color they are, mm-hum? You didn't know that drugs were so prevalent in all the schools, did you?"

He looked surprised and answered quietly, "No."

For the next two hours, Deron, Jeff and I talked about life. We discussed how life's problems can come dressed in a suit or in dirty clothes. It didn't matter what kind of wrapper they came in; they were still problems.

The boys told me that many of the kids at school had divorced parents; they too had seen drugs and alcohol abused at home, just as Deron and Jeff had. I must admit I was surprised. We'd never heard such things about this presumably fine suburban school or seen it reported on TV. Had it been an inner city school, we'd have heard all the bad reports—how tough the environment was and how the school had to install metal detectors and hire security guards. Well, guess what? There were security guards at this school too. And I was astonished to learn they had a drug rehabilitation program.

I had never in my life encountered such disrespectful teens as when I met some of the young men Deron liked to hang out with. These kids were no different from the ones in Denver; they did exactly what they wanted, whenever they wanted. They just did it behind the backs of the adults. I told Deron and Jeff that the only difference between these young men and them was that these kids had a better chance of getting a job without a degree than they did.

"You can play the same games," I told them, "but don't expect the same treatment—especially without a high school or college education."

ℙ

For many weeks, we spent our evenings talking for hours—especially on Thursdays, which were Mark's choir rehearsal nights. Often I came home from work much too tired for these marathon sessions. *I'm not going to say anything tonight,* I'd think. *I'm just going to bed!* But as soon as I walked through the door, it was like going into fifth gear. I received new energy from on high, and our rap sessions would last from 6:00 to 9:30 p.m. or later.

The boys would look at me with such intensity as I talked to them from the bottom of my heart. In my spirit, I thanked God for giving me such energy—and I praised Him whenever the boys opened up in response to my questions. Deron was often unsure what to say; he knew right from wrong but was so used to choosing wrong that many times his responses made absolutely no sense.

"Man, what are you saying?" Jeff would ask—and Deron would just laugh it off. Jeff had a lot of sense. He's blessed with both street smarts and book smarts. But many times he held himself back to keep from outshining his brother.

When Jeff came back to live with us, he began making C's in school. The previous year in Colorado, his report card had read "no effort." Obviously, Jeff was easily influenced, and his attitude toward school was a product of his surroundings. When we got his very first grade report, I knew he must be happy where he was. His grades were always a reflection of his happiness.

Basketball was all Jeff ever talked about. I made an agreement with him that if he would maintain a B average, he could play basketball as much as he wanted. A B average might seem high, but Jeff was capable of achieving straight A's. He hadn't come close to realizing his full potential.

When Jeff made the basketball team, I couldn't have been more proud of him. He too was proud and excited about playing. But once he made the team, he thought he could relax. This created another challenge for Mark and me. We wanted him to have fun, but Jeff needed to understand the discipline involved in staying on a team. If we didn't teach him, who would? We discovered that it's very hard to punish kids who have never had anything. If we said "no more television," so what? They'd rarely had access to a TV anyway. There was absolutely nothing to use as a source of punishment—not even housecleaning! Deron loved to help with the cleaning and did a great job at it.

♉

Several months passed before we made contact with the boys' mother. We never got good news about her well-being; she was always in and out of jail. Deron and Jeff rarely expressed how they felt about their mom, but I always reminded them to love and pray for her and her boyfriend. Weeks would go by, and they never asked about her. But when they finally talked to her, they often exaggerated how they were doing in school. Especially Jeff! You would have thought he was a straight A student!

During this time, Deron continued to hang out with the wrong crowd at school. We were taking it a day at a time with him. He didn't like school, and he began to lose ground—even in drama, the class he enjoyed most.

♉

"Mark, I'm still at work, but I got a message from the drama department. They were really upset. Deron didn't show up for rehearsal, and the performance is tomorrow night. I don't know what's wrong with him, but I'm tired of his games. I'm going up to the school to wait for him."

"Well, René, I'll meet you at home, and we can ride together," Mark said.

When we got to the school, we went straight to the auditorium where we were greeted by the drama teacher. "Mr. B" was a short, plump man with a pleasant personality. He always had a warm smile, and you could tell he really loved the kids.

"Hi, Mr. B. Is Deron here yet?" I asked.

"No."

"Well, we're going to wait for him."

We waited...and waited. Mr. B was very accommodating, and he thanked us for taking an interest in Deron. "Many parents don't take such an interest," he said.

After sitting there for awhile, we decided to search the school building. We poked around for an hour or so, but still no Deron. Then we got in the car and drove around for 30 minutes, up and down the nearby streets, in and out of strip malls—wherever we thought we might find him. Finally we went back to the school, where we sat for another hour.

I asked Mr. B whether they had an understudy for Deron's part in the show. "I don't think he'll be attending the play," I said, my embarrassment growing. By this time Mark and I were frustrated, exhausted and fairly angry. We decided to go home. Mr. B said he would call us if Deron showed up. *Deron is probably the only black kid in that drama class,* I remember thinking. *I don't know why he doesn't see what a bad example he's setting for his brother and any other young blacks at the school.*

At home, Mark and I had barely enough time to take off our coats before the phone rang. It was Mr. B, informing us that Deron was at the school. We thanked the teacher and asked him to keep Deron there. Then we went back to pick him up and drove home in shame.

Deron told us he had been down by the weight room, which was an absolute lie. We had checked the weight room thoroughly because he had used that excuse once before. It had been locked, and not one person was found nearby.

"So where were you, Deron?" I asked.

"I was by the weight room, and then I went outside."

"Where outside?"

"In the field."

"Deron, you're not telling the truth and I won't have it. Why in the world would you be out in a field? What were you doing? Getting high?"

"No."

I began to raise my voice.

"Well, what were you doing?" I said.

"Nothing. Just relaxing," he replied.

"All right. Just keep messing up and you'll relax all right. You've let your drama class down. They were counting on you for tomorrow night. Do you realize that?"

"Yeah."

"Why all of a sudden have you decided to make wrong choices?"

"I just didn't feel like staying after school, so I left."

"What do you mean you didn't feel like it?" I tried to explain to Deron that he'd made a commitment. In fact, it was he who had begged to be allowed in that class, who had agreed to do whatever it took. "You owe Mr. B an apology," I said. "Actually, you owe the entire class an apology."

There was no reaction from Deron.

"I will not have you lying to us the way you do," I continued. "I'd rather you tell me the truth, no matter how bad it is. Mark and I tell you the truth; we've never lied to you as long as you've known us! Do you realize what we're doing to try to help you get on the right track? Nothing worth having in life will come to you if you keep taking the easy way out."

After that, Deron really began to slack off, and his grades dropped drastically. He stayed out later and later in the evening. We had many sleepless nights. When Deron came home, he made up lame excuses. Sometimes I couldn't believe how shallow they were.

"Deron, did they change the time school lets out?"

"No. I was walking home and got lost," he replied.

"Lost?" I exclaimed, shaking my head. *This kid must think I'm crazy!* "You've been walking home the last five months, and today you got lost? I guess you could get lost if you're high. Why are your eyes so red?"

"I have allergies."

"You'll just say anything but the truth. You know I know what you're doing. But Deron, you're not hurting me! You're hurting yourself. And besides, no matter how hard you try to fool me, God sees and knows everything. Whatever you're doing, it will soon come to light!"

P

One time I asked Deron why he did the things he did.

"Because I don't want to forget my past," he arrogantly replied.

"Let me make sure I understand. You don't want to forget your past, so you continue to act in a way that will lead your life down a road of destruction?"

He nodded in agreement.

"Well, you don't have to forget your past, but you shouldn't want to live in the past. Anyway, you're not the only somebody with a past. What family do you think I come from? I tell you all the time about things that happened in our family—things I can't forget! Those things inspire me not to want to live in the past. I remember the past, but only to know where I want to go in the future. Your problem is you're stuck, and you can't move forward because you're feeling sorry for yourself."

I tried to remind Deron how blessed he was. So what if he once lived in the ghetto! He was alive, intelligent and a true survivor. By choice, he had missed a whole year of school the year before. But now he was in one of the nation's top school districts, making passing grades.

"Anything could have happened to you," I said. "You could be in a gang or in jail, but for some reason God has kept His hand on you. He has a great plan for your success. But it's easier to say you'd rather take than work to pay for what you want. I'm trying to help you get your priorities straight. Then you can enjoy a peaceful life. Stop trying to lead your own life, and ask Jesus to open your heart so that He can enter and help you make the right choices."

He didn't understand anything about Jesus.

𝔓

Sometimes I tried another approach with Deron.

"If you don't care about getting a high school degree, what I say will never matter. But you say you want to be a rapper. Let me see your work!"

He looked at me again with those great big eyes. It

was clear he had nothing to show.

"That's what I suspected," I said. "Well then, start writing. You think you can just start rapping? It's a business. You see the fun side of the business—being on stage, the girls, the crowds, the gold chains, the money. You seem to forget there's work involved in making it. Besides, what makes you think those guys don't have high school and college degrees?"

I could tell he was thinking about that one.

"Boy, you'd better wake up and get with the program," I went on. "I think you say you want to be a rapper because it goes against how I personally feel about a lot of rap music. Not all rappers rap about drugs, girls and living a dog's life."

"But—but that's my life," he interrupted.

"Does that mean your life is the right life? Do you really want kids selling drugs and calling girls "B's" and disrespecting females? Don't you know anything positive?"

"Yeah."

"Just think! You're here because your mom chooses to live the life you don't want to give up. Do you want your kids to go through the same thing?"

"I'm not gonna have kids," he said.

"Why?" I asked.

"Because I don't want any."

"I'll bet you have a real answer. You just won't share it."

Knowing better than to press for an answer, I told Deron I wanted him to understand that it was OK to live a life that didn't involve a struggle. He just turned away. I doubt he wanted to believe in what must have seemed impossible.

Chapter 11
Friday Nights

My sister, Lisa, was my pipeline to the latest information on the boys' mother. Our Thursday night phone conversations covered many topics, but sooner or later I always found a way to ask about Monica.

"Hey, Lisa, what's going on?"

"Nothing." Her usual answer. "Mr. Goree ain't doing so good."

"What's wrong?"

"He's old, girl, but he won't give up. He still tries to make it to Miss Esther's. He's got a cold he can't get rid of, and nobody will help him but me."

"What do you mean, nobody will help?"

"Girl, our daddy can't do too much of nothing anymore. I go over to make sure he's eating and that his apartment is clean. You wouldn't believe how Mr. Goree is going down. The doctor said he has fluid around his heart. His feet are so swollen he can hardly walk. They may have to put him in the hospital. The only one he'll go to is the V.A."

"Why is that?" I asked.

"I don't know," she replied. "I think he needs to see another doctor. He hates it when I leave him."

"Well, Lisa, God will bless you for what you're doing. I know it's hard, but God will give you strength. Have you heard from Monica?"

Lisa gave a deep sigh and said, "No, girl, Monica is too much."

"I know. We just have to pray for her. How's every-body else?"

We went through our usual Thursday night lineup, talking about how all our brothers and sisters were doing. As always, I shared something about how the boys were getting along, and then we said goodbye.

For a few minutes, my mind would replay parts of our conversation, and then I'd find myself thinking about the boys again—wondering what plight we'd be dealing with next. It would be Deron, of course.

"Well, Mark, Friday is coming," I said one night as we got ready for bed. "I hope and pray Deron comes home from school this time. He's done so well since we last talked, but I don't know. I have a feeling he won't be coming home this Friday." Throughout the week, Deron usually had no problem coming straight home from school. But he and his friends thought of Friday as party time.

For Mark and me, Friday was the night of our weekly Bible study with friends from church. For the past several years, we had gathered with the Wendell's and the Hamilton's to study God's Word. Mark and I were truly blessed that these couples agreed to open their hearts to help us study and grow in the Lord.

"Where are we having Bible study tonight?" I asked Mark the next morning.

"They said they'd come over here since we probably need to keep an eye on the boys."

That afternoon my suspicions were proven correct. Deron didn't come home from school. While we were studying that evening, my mind frequently drifted off; I wondered where Deron might be and why he kept making such wrong choices. No matter how many times he stepped on my heart, I always felt sorry for him. *This is a kid who is so hurt by life that the only way he knows how to cope is with drugs and alcohol,* I thought. *He refuses to accept the fact that he doesn't have to handle his problems by himself. God would do all the hard work for him, if he'd only let Him!*

We finished Bible study around 10:45 p.m. Jeff was upstairs watching videos. Every now and then, we'd hear him laughing out loud. He seemed to enjoy being a kid.

We continued to fellowship with the group for another hour. Our friends were also very concerned about Deron. But when the time came for them to leave, there was still no sign of him. Mark and I got in the car and drove around looking for him. We felt foolish knowing that no matter how hurt we were, Deron was having his fun. Heartbroken, we went home and went to bed. I could only pray that the Lord would keep Deron and give us strength to handle yet another trial.

𝔓

As my eyes opened to a new morning, I remembered that Deron had not come home the night before. I jumped out of the bed and ran to the window. To my surprise—

"Mark...*Mark!*"

"What's wrong?" he said, coming out of a deep sleep. It was only 6:00 a.m.

"Here he comes!"

Mark and I watched as this lost soul came walking down our street, wearing a hooded sweat top that was not his own. He was moving very slowly, his eyes pointed downward and the hood concealing his face from our view.

When he reached the house, he had the nerve to ring the doorbell. I opened the door.

"Why did you ring the bell?" I asked him.

"I lost my key."

"Boy, the nerve of you coming in here after being out all night and disobeying Mark and me! What's wrong with you?"

"Nothing." His face was expressionless.

"Yeah, something is wrong. When I tell you that you can't stay out all night and you do it anyway, something is definitely wrong. And you mean to tell me that the people you hang out with won't even give you a ride home? Where have you been?"

He looked me right in the eye and said, "Nowhere. I just stayed outside."

"Deron, I'm not crazy. I've told you again and again that you're messing up your own life, not mine. Is this really the kind of life you want to live?"

He just looked at me and shrugged his shoulders.

"I'm telling you, Deron, I'm not going to put up with it. You won't go to counseling, and you don't understand how important it is to have a relationship with Jesus Christ. He is the key to your having victory over needing to have stuff like drugs and alcohol in your body."

Just then the phone rang. It was the Hamilton's. They were concerned about Deron since he had not come home by the time they'd left the night before. I shared what had happened, and Pat encouraged me to take Deron to see a drug counselor in Leavenworth.

"I'm willing to try anything to shake some sense into this boy's head," I said. Though I didn't tell Pat, I also was afraid that Mark had had enough of Deron's disobedience. My husband had been very patient, but he had opened his heart and his home to two young men who didn't seem to care about either.

That afternoon Pat and I took Deron to see the counselor. On the way to Leavenworth, he barely said five words. I knew he was afraid and embarrassed, but he had built such a thick wall around him that no one could break through to him.

The counselor tested Deron and identified him as someone who wasn't motivated. He also said Deron had a violent personality and was capable of striking someone.

We already knew Deron wasn't motivated, but he was very mild tempered around us. I couldn't imagine him fighting and had never worried about him hitting me. Sometimes he talked about having liked to push people around in Denver; he said it made him feel good. But he wasn't that way around us.

On the ride home, Deron seemed more relaxed. He smiled and even sighed with relief. *He expected it to be worse,* I thought. *He must have thought we were going to leave him there.*

When we arrived home, I thanked Pat for her kind gesture. She and her husband knew what Mark and I were going through; they too had tried to raise a child who refused to accept their love. I also felt better having talked to a professional about Deron. *Maybe things will change now,* I told myself.

Deron was tired and still quite dirty from his all-nighter. It's amazing how partying all night can wear the human body down. Deron was barely 15 years old, but he looked about 20. There were bags under his eyes, his clothes were filthy and it even looked as if his nails had grown long. All of this had occurred in just one night.

"You need to go upstairs and clean yourself up," I said. "Why don't you take a good look at yourself in the mirror, and ask yourself if that's really how you want to look the rest of your life."

ℙ

Mark was so disappointed in Deron that he hardly knew how to respond.

"René, that boy knows exactly what he's doing! I know one thing. I'm the only man in this house, and if he wants to do whatever he wants, he'll have to leave."

"Mark, I know. But he doesn't know any better."

"Yeah, right!" Mark retorted. "Well, it's the life he knows, and for him it's fine to stay out and party all night. It was OK in Denver, but he's not in Denver anymore. He lives with us now, and not once has he seen us party or stay out all night!" Mark was furious.

"Mark, he can't change overnight," I said in Deron's

defense.

"I know that, but it hasn't been overnight. It's been several months!"

I gave a big sigh and said, "Let's just pray. If the Lord wants him somewhere besides here, we'll know in time."

❡

I desperately wanted Deron to become a positive role model for his brother. In Jeff's eyes, he was already a hero. Deron had raised Jeff to the best of his ability, and the younger boy looked up to him for guidance and protection.

That night I asked Jeff what he thought about Deron's behavior.

"How does it make you feel when your brother acts the way he does?"

Jeff, who always looked anywhere except my eyes, quietly replied, "I don't know. Just worried. He acted like that a lot in Denver."

"Did you act like that too?"

"No. I'd stay over at a friend's house because we didn't have anything to eat and my mom was never home. I didn't want to be home by myself. Deron didn't care. He'd stay gone for days."

"What would your mom say?"

"She'd tell him not to do it, but he did it anyway. I didn't like to go with Deron because his friends were really mean. Deron started treating me mean like his friends." I could hear the hurt in his voice. My heart could only take so much.

"Well, Jeff, just be thankful God protected you through all of that stuff. Do you understand what I'm saying?"

He nodded.

"You see, after all you and your brother have been through, God didn't let you die of starvation. You may not have had much of anything, but through it all you're still standing. You've got good health. God has kept you and your brother. Be thankful. All that you went through should make you a better person. I just want you to know two things."

It was always hard to tell whether Jeff was really listening. Unlike Deron, he never looked me in the eyes. Deron looked me in the eyes, but he still did exactly what he wanted to do. I could only pray that one day the things I was telling them would strike them both like lightning.

"The first thing I want you to know is that we love you. You don't have to be ashamed because you had to come and live with your aunt and uncle. Just because you lived in a bad neighborhood doesn't mean you're bad or that others are better than you. Where do you think I grew up?"

"Denver," he said, his voice slightly louder than a whisper.

"Right. In Denver in the projects."

"Projects?" he asked.

"'Projects' are what they call a housing division. It's only a name. Now, what we did as a people was choose to make that name bad. We could have made it good! I don't care what folk say. Just because you live in low-income housing doesn't mean you have to let such a stereotype live in you. But we got so caught up in the name that we allowed society to convince us that the word 'projects' means 'no hope.' You have to remember your favorite Scripture, Philippians 4:13. You must believe that you can do all things through Jesus Christ, who strengthens you. That's where your hope is reassured. Do you understand what I'm saying?" Surprisingly, he did.

"Yes!" he said with confidence.

"The same thing goes for life," I told him. "You choose how you want to live. That's why when you pray for your mom, it's important that you understand that no matter how long God knocks at the door of her heart, He'd rather be invited in than come in uninvited. God gives us a choice."

I could tell Jeff was tired of hearing me preach. We were all tired; Deron had kept us all up pretty late the night before. But I had one more thing to say.

"Jeff, the second thing I want you to know is that when no one else in this world seems to love you, you can know that God loves you. He loves you more than you love yourself, no matter what your situation in life may be."

He may not have understood my words then, but I prayed he was storing them in his memory bank.

𝓟

Later that evening, Mark and I sat in his office, which was across the hall from the boys' room. When we asked Deron to come in and talk with us, his face showed no sign of remorse.

"Deron, is there something you need to say?"

He shrugged his shoulders as if to say "not really."

"Well, Deron, you need to say something. You can't walk around here like everything is OK."

"What do you want me to say?"

"I want you to say whatever is on your heart. Don't tell us what you think we want to hear."

"Ummmm, I—" he began, "I know y'all don't want me to stay out, but I like having fun."

We thought Deron would understand that he was supposed to apologize for his behavior, but he still didn't get it. We had to deal with him on his level.

"Deron, can't you see it worries us when we don't know where you are? Even if you call and say, 'I'm over at so-and-so's house, is it OK if I stay a little later?' We may say yes or no. But you're only 15, and you owe us that respect. What you are doing is something only grown folks are privileged to do. Are you grown?"

"No."

"Can you get a job by yourself or live on your own?"

"No."

"That's right. What I'm saying is that you're too young to try to live like an adult—and too young to do whatever you want because you don't feel like being obedient."

"OK, I'll try to do better," he said. It was obvious he wanted to end the conversation.

"Deron, I think that's your problem. You're always trying. Make a commitment to actually do it instead of trying. When you tell yourself to try, you leave room for a cop-out. Tell yourself you'll do it instead!"

"No, because I might not do it," Deron replied, clearly confused.

Oh goodness, he still doesn't get it. I prayed for words that would shatter the thick, hard shell that kept him from hearing.

"Let me explain something. If you doubt your abilities, you'll never succeed. You like rap—better yet, you love rap! Do you think you'll ever be a rapper?"

"I don't know. I'm gonna try." Still he refused to commit.

"Do you think your idol Tupac said he was going to try? You've got to say, 'I will.' Have you ever heard about the little red train that could?"

"No," he said with a smirk.

I told him the story of how the little train became "the little train that could," once the train began believing in its own potential. All along, the train had an engine; it just didn't know how powerful that engine was.

"Guess what, Deron?"

"What?"

"You have an engine too. I don't take you to Sunday school for nothing. I want you to learn about your "engine," Jesus Christ. That little red train was trying to make it up the hill without starting his engine. In everything you do, don't forget to start your engine."

"I'll put it another way. If you went out to the garage and sat in the car, would it move?" Now I was really trying to break it down for him.

For a minute Deron looked excited, as if I was going to let him drive.

"Don't think about it, buddy! Answer my question. Would the car start?"

"No!"

"Why not?"

"Because you have to start it up." He said it proudly as he read my expression of relief. *Finally, a right answer!*

"Thank you, Deron. You know, I love you and I won't watch you throw your life away. I'm responsible for you and your brother. How do you feel physically after you've stayed out all night drinking and getting high?"

He thought about it for a moment. "Um, tired," he said.

"I know you do. You're tearing your body down before you've built it up. Deron, you owe it to yourself to get your life together. I can't do it for you. Neither can Mark, your mom or Jeff. Besides, don't you want your own family one day?"

"I don't know. I probably just want to live with somebody," he said.

In times like these, I always had two conversations going at the same time—an audible one with the boys, and an inaudible one with Jesus. *Lord, please have mercy,* I said to Him now.

"Deron, do you mean you'd love a young lady enough to live with her, but wouldn't marry her?" I don't think Deron wanted to have any morals at all; he always desired the opposite of what was right. He refused to answer my question.

"What if you have kids?" Mark asked.

"I'll probably get married."

I knew that my nephew needed much prayer. He thought like a child who had never been taught to do what pleases God. All of his thoughts simply sprang from what he was used to seeing. His mom wasn't married and had men in and out of her apartment all the time. We didn't even know who the boys' fathers were. How else was Deron to think?

It was long past our bedtime, but I needed to ask him one more question.

"Deron, would you ever hit a woman?"

"No."

"I pray not."

Then out of the blue Deron said, "I think you guys give me too much attention."

"What?" *Where did this come from?*

With his usual smirk, he repeated what I thought he had said, adding, "It's just that I think I can do better if you don't pay me any attention."

145

"Deron, the problem is that it's not the kind of attention we want to give you. Do us a favor; help us not have to give you any attention!"

"OK, I will. You'll see, I'm gonna do better." He said it with confidence. Mark and I exchanged hopeful glances. *Maybe we finally got through!*

ℙ

Deron's quest to do the right thing lasted about two weeks.

"You've been doing really well and I'm proud of you, " I told him on a Friday morning before school. "Now don't be influenced by your friends after school today. Do the right thing. Remember, He that is in you is greater than he that is in the world!"

On the way home from work that afternoon, I didn't make my usual call to find out whether Deron had come home. Afraid of what I might find, I didn't even hurry to get home. After taking the longest route possible, I finally pulled into the garage.

"Jeff, where's your brother?" I said coming into the house. My mind was so preoccupied with Deron that I forgot to ask Jeff how he was doing.

"I don't know. He didn't come home after school today."

"I don't believe that boy," I said. "Every time I try to encourage him, he screws up."

ℙ

We all went about our evening. I knew that eventually Deron would be sauntering in with some lie on his lips. Boy, was I ever right! The doorbell rang around 11:00 p.m. When I opened the door, there was Deron, standing in the bitter cold, breathing hard as if he had been running.

"What's wrong with you, Deron?"

"It's the police! The police are after me!"

My heart began to race.

"What? Slow down! What are you saying?"

"The police! They're after me!"

I looked up and down the street. The neighborhood was quiet.

"Nobody's after you, Deron. What have you been doing?"

"Nothing! It's the police!"

By this time, I was up in his face, looking him square in the eye. He reeked of liquor.

"Deron, are you drunk?"

"No."

"Yes, you are—now, stop your lying! You mean to tell me your friends can take you out and get you drunk, and they can't even give you a ride home?" He blew right past my questions, still wanting to talk about the police.

"Drop it, Deron. There are no police. I'm not crazy, and if you insist on being disobedient, you cannot stay here."

Inside, my heart was bleeding. Sooner or later, I'll

have to mean what I say, I reminded myself. I couldn't continue to subject Mark and our home to such blatant disrespect.

"I don't know where you're going, but you will not stay here drunk. Not tonight! Jeff, get your cousin Brian on the phone and let me speak with him."

That night, as he had several times before, Brian came to pick up Deron because I wouldn't allow such chaos in our home. *Thank You for Brian,* I prayed. Without him, I don't know what I would do.

The next morning Deron returned home as if nothing had happened. I had my usual talk with him. He went through the motions of listening, but he and I both knew it would only be a matter of days before the next disturbance. Christmas was just around the corner, and Deron's punishment was that he would receive no Christmas gift. He had asked for a gold chain, which I purchased and placed neatly on the Christmas tree. I informed him of where it was and told him that he could have it as a birthday gift on January 24—depending on how he chose to act between now and then.

Christmas was a solemn day, as Deron sat quietly and watched his brother open his gifts. For the next few weeks, we all cheered him on—hoping and praying that he would stay clean until his birthday. I believe we wanted him to have that gold chain as much as he wanted it.

"Mark, it looks like somebody is going to get a gold chain tomorrow," I said in a voice loud enough for everyone to hear. Deron looked up from the dining room table with a smile. We were all happy, mostly because Deron had proven he knew right from wrong. He was making good choices—and we were all finally getting some rest!

The next morning I was too excited to wait any longer. I awoke Deron and told him how proud of him we were. As I placed the gold chain around his neck, I said that I prayed he would always continue to make the right choices in life.

But it wasn't long before Deron returned to his old ways. As our conflicts with him escalated, we began to ask the members of our church family to pray. Many of them still pray for Deron and Jeff, and I believe it's the prayers of the righteous that keep them safe.

Some weeks were better than others, but it was becoming hard to deal with the constant strife he caused in our home. Deron required so much attention that it was almost unfair to Jeff. And Mark couldn't understand how or why I allowed this kid to run our lives.

I continued to talk to Deron about choices. His unwillingness to listen began to tire me out. The only thing that kept me going was that God had never given up on me. The difference is, I had a willing spirit. Deron wasn't ready or willing to hear about Christ, who could have placed his feet on a rock and established his ways.

My bark was losing its bite. Deron didn't seem to care. Whatever I said, his response was that he used to be worse in Denver. Mark and I began to argue about Deron's disrespectful behavior. Mark was tired of hearing Deron apologize time after time. "Perhaps since he thinks we're going to keep him until he's 18, he feels he can treat us any way he wants," Mark speculated.

My husband's misgivings made me wonder if perhaps Deron would be better off somewhere else. I began talking to him about joining the military. But Deron told me he was afraid to go into the service because he might get killed. I just shook my head, unable to fathom how he could join a gang and be willing to die for another gang member, yet fear getting killed in the service. It's amazing how we pigeonhole tough kids, thinking they don't care about life. Try talking to a kid's inner spirit, and you'll learn otherwise. I can't imagine how many fears Deron dealt with on a daily basis—fears he always masked as a means of survival.

Mark and I continued to pray for wisdom, and by the grace of God, I never became discouraged with the Lord. I knew the boys were with us for a reason. We just needed to trust Him.

Chapter 12
Tell the Truth

When school let out for the summer, I immediately sent Deron on a job search. This time I wanted him to gain the experience of finding a job on his own. He had recently turned 16, and as he approached adulthood, there were so many basic life skills he needed to learn.

I was proud of Deron as he took the initiative in applying for full-time positions at several department stores. But without my help, nothing seemed to pan out. I finally decided I'd better get involved. One afternoon I took Deron to a local sandwich shop, spoke with the manager, and Deron was hired on the spot—I believe because the manager trusted my word when I vouched for Deron's character. That same day we took Jeff to a McDonald's in the same shopping center. He too was hired on the spot.

Deron really liked to work. "If work were all that boy had to do, our lives would be a lot easier," I often commented to Mark. We were grateful that both boys seemed to enjoy making their own money.

When they began working, we taught both Deron and Jeff to first give God His tithe, then put half their income in the bank. The remainder was theirs to spend as they pleased. The boys were always competing with one another, trying to see who could make more money than his brother.

Looking back, it was a fairly good summer. Deron enjoyed working, and from all appearances, he seemed to go the entire summer without drinking or getting high.

Although we were thrilled, we wondered how he could stay drug-free all summer, yet succumb to temptation so easily during the school year. Was the influence of his friends that strong?

ᚦ

Mark and I purchased a caller I.D. unit for our phones. Deron and Jeff were unaware that we'd added this feature since we kept the box in our bedroom. That summer, we began noticing many calls from a local rehabilitation center. When we asked Deron who was calling, he told us that a friend of his was getting treatment for drug and alcohol abuse.

My mind started running a mile a minute. *Is it really true that birds of a feather flock together? Does this mean Deron is using again? Now, wait just a minute, René. Give that boy the benefit of the doubt; at least he's getting treatment. Yeah, but Deron's hanging out with the wrong sort of person. He's not strong enough to help himself; how can he be strong enough to help that young man? Lord, have mercy!*

I had known several people who had gone through drug rehab, and none of them had managed to maintain any distance from friends who continued to use. For some reason, they made it their mission to try to save their friends. The sad thing is, none of these individuals was ever strong enough to carry out this mission.

I was convinced that Deron needed friends who had other interests and could provide the right kind of encouragement. Was the boy in the rehab center strong enough to discourage Deron's drug use—or would he encourage my nephew to fall back into his old habits? I didn't know.

Growing up, I was taught not to hang out with disrespectful kids or those who had bad habits. Ma-Dear so embedded this in my mind that I was always cognizant of the company I kept—so much so that my friends who may have cursed, gotten high or smoked cigarettes never dreamed of inviting me to do so! The funny thing is, I never told those kids that I wouldn't do those things. They just never asked! I now believe that God was sheltering me from evil, long before I ever realized it. Without His divine protection, I could have made so many wrong decisions.

℘

We learned that the boy in rehab was named Don. He had his own car and was very much into rap. He often came by the house, and Deron always talked to him on the front porch. After he'd stopped by a couple of times, I went out to introduce myself and invited him inside. I always asked the boys' friends how they were doing in school, what they wanted to grow up to be and if they believed in Jesus. They always told me exactly what I wanted to hear.

Deron had another friend named Bret; we didn't know whether he was a junior or a senior. Like Deron, he too lived with his aunt and uncle. This young man was really into girls—and to us, he seemed very sneaky. In fact, we didn't trust him one bit.

We met Bret's uncle under the most awkward circumstances. Instead of coming home one evening after work, Deron spent the night at Bret's house. Naturally, we didn't know where he was. The next morning he called and told us he'd fallen asleep in Bret's basement on the couch. I asked to speak with the aunt or uncle—and when Bret's uncle came to the phone, he told me he had no idea Deron was even in the house! He said his nephew had come upstairs to speak with him but never mentioned that a friend was there. *Deron and Jeff better not have somebody in our basement and I don't know about it!* I thought. *Maybe that's the problem, that we trust kids too much these days. There's no telling what they were doing in that basement!*

Bret's uncle brought Deron home; since it was Saturday morning and I had a hair appointment, Mark had the honor of meeting him. Mark later told me that Bret's uncle was very nice and that he'd just purchased a used car for his nephew. Friends with cars meant even more opportunity for Deron to hang out away from home. I tried to give the boys' friends the benefit of the doubt, but I couldn't ignore their potential impact on my nephews.

"Deron's friend, Eric, isn't a bad kid," I told Mark, trying not to be judgmental. "He seems to be influencing Deron to do more positive things. They're talking about making a tape. Supposedly he has a system in his basement."

Mark looked at me as if that was the craziest thing I could possibly say. But somehow I believed that if the boys could expend their energies doing something constructive or focus on specific goals, perhaps the desire for drugs would disappear.

❧

"I heard Donna is sending Carl to stay with Brian," I said to Mark one day early in the summer. Carl was Brian's younger brother, and Donna must have thought that Brian would be a positive role model for his sibling. Brian was such a respectful young man. Like most young guys, he had made some mistakes, but he worked every day and took good care of his family.

Every now and then, Brian would come and get the boys. Deron enjoyed going to Brian's house more than Jeff did. Jeff tended to feel left out whenever Deron hung out with his friends or his cousins. Brian also liked to listen to rap, which was right up Deron's alley. The difference was, rap music didn't seem to influence Brian as it did Deron. Deron absolutely loved the hard core, woman-degrading rap—the kind we didn't allow in our home.

Not long ago, we had a special youth service at our church, and the pastor commented that we gave our sons guns to play with, and now they're killing each other. We gave our daughters baby dolls, and now teenage pregnancy is uncontrollable. He reminded us that we must be very careful what we give our children. The very things we once thought were cute are the very things keeping parents awake at night.

❧

After a few weeks in the city, Carl came over to spend the weekend with the boys.

"What do you guys want to do today?" I asked the

three of them. "Carl, you're our guest today. What do you want to do?"

"Well, Eric's coming over and we're going with him," Deron interjected.

"Um-hum. Going where with him?"

"Over to his house to practice our rap."

"Do his parents know you're coming over?"

"He said they didn't mind."

"Are you sure? Maybe I need to call them. You know I like to introduce myself to your friends' parents, so if something happens I know who to contact."

There was complete silence as the boys exchanged glances.

"What time is Eric supposed to be here?" I asked.

"In about an hour," said Deron.

"All right. You all get ready so I can hear you rap before you leave."

It didn't take a mind-reader to know what they were thinking: *Why is she doing this to us?*

"You said you were rappers, right?" I said.

"Yes," they replied in unison.

"Well, what I'm asking shouldn't be a problem then. I can't wait to hear my nephews rap!"

In an hour or so, Eric rang the doorbell.

"He's here!" called out Jeff.

"Good, let him in. Hi, Eric," I said.

"Hi," he practically whispered. *Kids today crack*

me up, acting so big and tough. This one can't even speak up!

"Deron told me you guys are going to make a tape."

"Uh, yeah. We've got all the information."

"You do?"

"Yeah." *Never "yes." Just "yeah."* "We've been going to the studio," he told me.

"What studio?" *There's no telling where these kids are while we're at work!* I said to myself.

"A studio over in Missouri." Missouri was a different state, but it was really just a half-hour's drive from our home.

Deron, Jeff and Carl began to make a face at Eric like, You're talking way too much, man! Then everything began to come out—all the secrets my nephews had obviously hoped to keep from me.

"Um, yeah! Eric's been paying for our studio time, and he also paid $250 for our beats," said Deron.

"He paid what? What are beats?"

"Uh, you know," he said.

"No, I don't know, Deron. That's why I'm asking."

"You know, beats! It's the music you rap to."

"Well, let me hear the tape. Why did Eric pay for it, anyway?"

"We're going to pay him back," Jeff volunteered.

"How?"

"With the money we save from working this summer," he said.

"Eric, don't you let these boys cheat you out of your money," I warned. "And Deron, don't you guys make him pay for everything because that certainly is not right!" I hoped that Eric wasn't trying to buy the boys' friendship—but I also wanted to make sure Deron and Jeff weren't trying to pull a fast one on this kid. The way I saw it, their attitude was, Hey, we're street smart, and this guy's from Kansas. There's no way he can be cooler than we are! *Whatever the truth of the matter, kids will make you crazy,* I thought.

Mark and I listened to the beats, and to our surprise they were really smooth. I had imagined a lot of loud, harsh bass—at a tempo so intense it could cause a heart attack!

Then we asked the guys to rap for us. "Nothing derogatory and no curse words," we told them. Eric had no problem; he went right into his rap—and truth be known, he out-rapped Deron by a long shot. He was better at what they call "free-style," while Deron was more talented at writing. He couldn't free-style, but he rapped fairly well when he had the words in front of him.

𝓟

Summer was tough because Mark and I were gone every day. There were days when the boys didn't have to work or got off early. While they were at work, I could relax; at least I knew where they were. But when they were home, I couldn't help but worry. Deron and Jeff were too old for sitters, so we just had to trust them—and God knows it's hard to trust people who are known for being untrustworthy.

All we could do was pray, asking God to keep them in their right minds and out of trouble. Some days, I'd try to show up when they least expected it. They'd scramble to straighten up and act as if nothing was going on. I always looked at the stereo, knowing that if the stereo was on, they'd been jamming. That was really no big deal—but I would have preferred that they use the stereo openly, rather than sneak and play it, then pretend they were watching television when I walked in. What I really wanted was for them to be themselves.

𝓟

Our biggest problem that summer was the boys' failure to come home by the times we had set for them. Inevitably, they'd show up a couple of hours late—but in the meantime, I wore out the telephone lines trying to trace their steps.

"Hello?"

"Hi, this is René Parson, Deron's aunt. He and his brother left with your nephew Bret today, and I asked them to come home by 9:00 p.m. I was wondering if Bret made it home or if you knew where the boys were."

"No, Bret was supposed to work today," said the woman on the other end of the line. I noticed that her voice was very calm. "I wouldn't worry. They'll probably be in soon."

Well! I knew I sounded like a frantic parent, but her breezy, oh-don't-you-worry attitude made me doubly upset!

"Mark, these people are so carefree about how their

kids act. I can't believe it!" I vented to my husband. "Then again, who knows. Maybe they're right! We're here wringing our hands, worrying while Deron and Jeff are out having fun—not even thinking about us till it's time to walk through that door with some lie! But I don't know. I just can't let kids run my house and disobey the rules!"

A little later, the phone rang. *Now, who can this be,* I thought as I eyed the caller I.D. The number wasn't one we knew.

"Hello?"

"Hi, Aunt René. This is Deron."

"Where are you?"

"We're at a friend's house."

"What time did I tell you to come home?"

"Nine."

"Deron, it's almost 11:00 p.m.," I said, my frustration growing. "Get home right now."

I hung up the phone—then picked up the receiver again. Checking the caller I.D. unit, I dialed the same number and asked the young girl who answered if I could speak with her parents. The girl told me her parents weren't home and that she didn't know who Deron was. Obviously, she wasn't telling the truth.

Twenty minutes later, Deron and Jeff called from a pay phone.

"Why do you keep calling me?" I asked. "The next time I hear your voice, you'd better be in this house!"

Hanging up the phone, I turned to my husband.

"Mark, what are we doing wrong? They don't seem to understand that they can't be out there in these little hot-tailed girls' homes while their parents are away. As soon as something happens, guess who'll get blamed? All they'll say is that they didn't do it. I've got to help them see that they have to be careful about just hanging out."

<p>

Twenty minutes later, Deron, Jeff, Carl and Bret appeared at our door. Bret was the spokesperson, and he launched into an explanation that was pure fiction.

"Um, I just want you to know that it was my fault," he said at the conclusion of his speech.

Unemotionally, I replied, "Your fault? For what? For keeping them out late? I don't even want to hear it, young man, because I teach my nephews the difference between right and wrong. So, no, it's not your fault. They chose to stay out. Now, I'm going to ask that you go home—and if I'm not mistaken, you were supposed to be at work today and should have been home long before now."

He put on a pitiful expression as he let himself out the front door. I turned my attention to the other three boys.

"Carl, I'm surprised at you," I said. "I thought you would make the right decision." He had nothing to say for himself, and Deron and Jeff weren't talking either. Drained and defeated by yet another conflict, I fed the boys a snack and told them to go to bed. It didn't escape my notice that Deron had the munchies.

℘

I couldn't wait for summer to end so that the boys could get back to school. This pattern of staying out late was getting very tiresome.

One night after driving around town looking for the boys, I decided I'd had enough. As I pulled in front of my house, I rolled down my window to pick up the mail. That's when, out of the corner of my eye, I saw a car drop off two boys up the street. I looked again. *Yes, it's Deron and Jeff—but they haven't seen me!* I pulled into garage and dialed Mark's cell phone.

Mark was on his way home from choir rehearsal when he got my call.

"Mark, it was getting close to 10p.m., and I hadn't heard from Deron and Jeff all day, so I went out looking for them. I don't even know if Jeff went to work today."

I told Mark about seeing the car drop them off up the street. "They don't even know I saw them," I said. As I sat in the car talking to Mark, someone knocked on the window.

"Let me call you back," I told my husband as I rolled down the window.

"Hey, what's up?" Deron and Jeff stood nonchalantly beside the car. "Where are you coming from?" I asked.

"Playing basketball."

"You were?"

"Yeah, we were," said Jeff.

These kids were so easy to read; I could already tell

they were lying. I got out of the car, and the three of us went into the house.

"Where were you guys playing?" I asked.

"At T-Ridge." T-Ridge was the name of the neighborhood community center.

"Really? Well, where's your basketball?"

"Um, I d-d-didn't take it," said Jeff.

"Oh. I thought you always carried your ball with you. Well, who'd you play with?"

By this time, so much mumbling and stuttering was going on that the boys should have guessed I'd be on to their story. Besides, Deron was pacing the room.

"What's wrong, Deron?"

"Nothin'."

"Well, I'll give you both a chance to tell me the truth. You know I'd rather you tell me the truth than to lie."

Jeff started talking, spilling everything they had done that day. I could tell it made his brother angry.

"Shut up, man!" he shouted. "You don't know what you're talkin' about!"

Jeff kept talking and Deron got louder.

"I said, shut up!"

"Hey you, be quiet," I interjected. "As a matter fact, stop pacing and sit down! If you hadn't done anything wrong, you wouldn't be so mad. Now go give it a rest because I'm not ready to hear from you yet."

Steaming mad, Deron stalked out of the kitchen and slumped down on a couch in the family room.

"Now, Jeff, you guys have been lying to me all night. Why should I even listen to you?"

Jeff gave me his you-can-believe-me look—the one where he'd look me square in the eye and speak without stuttering. Whenever Jeff lied, he stuttered. All I wanted was for him to tell the truth—something they both had trouble doing.

Jeff finally told me that he and his brother had spent the evening hanging out at a couple of malls. They lied because they knew I wanted them to use their time doing something more productive than loitering at the mall. "Kids get in trouble just hanging out at malls," I often told them.

I thanked Jeff for being honest. After I'd said all I could think of to say, I went upstairs. It was really no big deal; all they had to tell me was the truth. The boys stayed downstairs and had an interesting conversation of their own—an exchange that tipped me off to the way they probably talked when Mark and I weren't around.

"Man, you're crazy!" Jeff said to Deron.

"No, I ain't. You should'a been quiet like I told you."

"Man, I told you René knew. She knows everything!"

I was perched at the top of the stairs, my ear squeezed between the banisters, straining to hear the "real" Deron and Jeff.

"She does not know everything," Deron argued.

"She knew about tonight, didn't she?" said Jeff.

Deron didn't respond.

"Man, you're gonna get us in trouble, and when they send us back to Denver, what will we do?" Jeff's words pierced my heart. But his brother's reply literally brought me to my knees.

"Ahh, mother f——r, I'll take care of myself."

I slumped on the floor above the stairwell, not believing I had heard my nephew curse like a sailor in my own home.

"How are you gonna take care of yourself when you can't?" Jeff asked.

"Man, you're crazy! You're just a little punk," Deron told him.

"You're not even listening to me, Deron. I'm not even gonna talk to you anymore." Whatever Deron's next words were, his brother tuned them out. I was proud of Jeff because in the entire conversation, he had never used one curse word or any foul language.

I've heard enough, I said to myself. *Now I truly know they know right from wrong. They can make sound decisions if they want to. No one is persuading them to do anything!*

Out of the blue, something told me to ask the boys for their bank cards.

"Hey, guys. Come up here, please!" I yelled from the top of the stairs.

I could feel the tension as they dragged themselves up the stairs. They probably guessed I had overheard their conversation, but I didn't mention it. *It's funny,* I thought. *When I heard Deron downstairs he sounded as if he'd just gotten out of prison and wasn't afraid of anybody!* Now he was coming up the stairs looking as meek as a puppy dog.

They both handed me their bank cards. As usual, it took awhile for me to get the truth out of the boys, but when I did, it confirmed what I suspected. Deron and Jeff had both taken money out of their accounts.

"You see, everything you do, I know about it," I told them. "When you do wrong, it always comes to light. Now, the money we put in your account is to help buy school clothes. From now on, I guess I'll have to hold on to your bank cards since I can't trust that you are responsible young men. And you weren't even going to tell me! When the time came to go shopping, you'd have told me some outrageous story."

I shook my head, disheartened by the events of the evening. "I'm tired of all this lying," I said. "You guys had better get it together. Do Mark and I lie to you?"

"No," said Jeff.

"Well, why do you lie to me?" Neither boy said a word. "I've told you guys that the Lord sent you here for a reason, and it's Mark's and my job to make sure we're in line with how He tells us to be good relative foster parents. That's why you won't get away with anything. God will show us everything you're doing."

For a fleeting moment, I saw the fear of God on

those boys' faces, as if they were thinking, *I don't want to mess with a God like that—who knows everything I do!*

"You should know by now that you don't get away with anything. The sad thing is, all I ask for is the truth. I can handle the truth much better than you deceiving yourselves—thinking you're getting away with something when you're not."

By now, Mark was home and it was time for bed. After an episode like that, it was always hard to unwind. And even if I did sleep, the night would be a restless one.

Chapter 13
The Final Chapter

The long summer finally reached an end. Mark and I decided to have Jeff quit his job when school started, but we allowed Deron to continue working. Deron seemed to enjoy his job, and this would give him something positive to do after school.

It's true when they say that a picture is worth a thousand words. One of my life's finest "Kodak moments" came when I took the boys to withdraw money from their bank accounts for their back-to-school shopping. Deron and Jeff had no idea the amount of money they'd saved over the summer, especially since we couldn't get them to keep a record in their little bank books. Deron had saved more than $400, and Jeff had slightly more than $300. Their hands were literally shaking as they took the cash from the teller.

On our way to the mall, Deron said it felt really good to go shopping with the money he had earned. I could tell he was proud that he didn't have to sell drugs or steal to buy school clothes. Jeff said he had never been given so much money at one time for clothes. The thing about those two is that it didn't take much to make them happy! For many kids today, $300 to $400 would be just enough for a pair of shoes.

I dropped the boys at the mall and told them to act like gentlemen. I cried all the way back to work, thinking about all they had been through. How proud of them I was! Just the fact that they were happy made me unbelievably happy too.

✆

We signed the boys up for their classes. This would be Jeff's first year in high school. I explained to him that people would already know him by his last name, for Deron didn't have a good reputation. Jeff listened as I told him he didn't have to be stereotyped by Deron's actions.

"You can change the reputation of your last name by doing things right," I said.

That night I said to Mark, "You know, I don't know if I can handle the both of them acting up like they did last year. I pray that this year is much better."

✆

Deron hadn't been in school a month before I got the first call from his assistant principal.

"Mrs. Parson? This is the assistant principal at the high school. I wanted to let you know that Deron was sent to the office today because his teacher thought she smelled marijuana on him. Deron said he'd been smoking cigarettes earlier this morning."

"Smoking cigarettes? I didn't know he smoked. Where is he now?"

"We sent him back to class."

Goodness, this boy hasn't been in school a good month, and already he's acting up, I thought to myself, almost forgetting there was someone on the phone line.

"Well, thank you for calling," I said to the principal. "I'll address the issue when Deron gets home."

That afternoon my first words to Deron were, "Deron, do you have something to tell me?"

"No—" he began.

What a surprise that answer was! Cutting short his lie, I asked, "Well, why did you have to go to the principal's office today?"

"Because I had a cigarette lighter." He already knew my next question. "This boy put it in my pocket," he said.

"Deron, that's pretty weak, buddy. You mean to say you let somebody get you into trouble?" By now my temperature had risen a few degrees. "Look, you will not drive me crazy this year. I'm going to Social Services tomorrow. We are going to have some kind of ground rules around here. I'm tired, Deron. You don't want counseling, and you don't want to do right in school. I can't help you if you don't want help. I don't even know what's important to you. What is important to you, Deron?"

Staring at me, he just shrugged his shoulders.

"I know you've been through a lot, but it's not right that you make my life so rough. You don't like church; you're just there. You won't make friends with the kids who want to live right—and I know everybody at that school doesn't ditch class and do drugs. This year you will make a choice, and if you choose to do nothing with your life, then maybe Mark and I can't help you. Last year was a year of hell—and I'm not living in hell this year."

"I'm sorry," Deron said.

"Deron, you don't mean it! 'I'm sorry, I'm sorry,

I'm sorry,' that's what you always say." I mimicked him in a mocking tone of voice. "Well, stop being sorry and start getting your life in order. You're a junior now. What's next?"

"I don't know."

"Why not?

"I don't know."

"Are you scared?" He shrugged his shoulders.

"I don't know."

"What do you know?"

"I know I care about my family."

"Who is your family?"

"Jeff, my mom, you and Mark."

"Well, if you care about us, why do you keep us in such turmoil?" He had no answer. "Deron, when you care about people, you do the right things. And if you know what hurts them, you stop doing those things. Your prayer to God is always that He stop your mom from doing drugs. Well, why do you ask?" Still no response. "Could it be it's because she's hurting you and your being able to be together as a family?"

"Yeah," he said.

"You're breaking my heart because you don't realize your potential. You are a very intelligent, handsome young man."

Deron just smiled and shook his head in disagreement.

"Deron, no matter how much I love you or tell you

how much possibility you have, you'll never have a break-through unless you believe it. It's your life, and God has given you a free will. You get to choose what type of life you want to live. It's not my choice; it's yours."

Before I knew it, the clock was striking 10:00 p.m. We had spent several hours talking. Jeff, who always sat in on my conversations with his brother, looked exhausted. The three of us prayed. I told them I loved them, and we all went to bed. *Now I know what it means to talk until you're blue in the face,* I thought as I nestled beneath the covers.

𝄢

I dreaded it, but as soon as Deron and Jeff were back in school, I resumed my routine of calling their teachers to check on their progress. I always received compliments from the teachers on how nice they were. Both boys were in the same art class—a good arrangement, I thought, except that it messed with Deron's ego. He pretended it didn't, but it was all an act.

Deron was also in a freshman swim class—a required class for graduation. On one of my phone calls, his teacher informed me that Deron was failing the class because he refused to suit up. She also stated that Deron wanted to drop the class. *What a confused system!* I thought. *It lets teens make adult decisions when they aren't yet capable of thinking like adults.* No child should be able to drop a class without a parent's consent. This school system allowed kids to drop classes without the parents' knowledge, but if they didn't return the books, at the end of the year the parents were still responsible for the cost. Go figure!

I made an appointment and went to meet with Deron's teacher. From the first moment, she and I hit it off really well. She told me about her 16-year-old son and that she understood what I was going through. She believed that Deron was having a self-esteem issue. He'd told her that his legs were too skinny to wear shorts—and that he felt a lot older than the kids in the class.

I had mixed emotions about that. While I felt sorry for Deron and wished he didn't have to take the class, I didn't want him to feel sorry for himself and just give up. The teacher also said that another kid was picking up Deron every day after class. Sometimes Deron would sneak out before class was over and leave with this boy.

The teacher and I worked to come up with several scenarios that would allow Deron to get caught up in this class. The key to everything was that he had to want it as badly as we did.

♇

After meeting with Deron's teacher, I finally knew why he came home late many evenings. He was supposedly staying after school, doing make-up work in several classes. In actuality, he was just hanging out.

Feeling I needed some intervention and support, I decided to call Social Services. I wanted S.R.S. to understand what was going on with the boys, but I also had another motive. Mark and I felt we needed to be careful since at-risk kids will often inflate their stories to the authorities, making it seem as if they're being mistreated. When kids are not, in fact, receiving fair treatment from their caregivers, I believe that corrective action should be taken. But this was not the case with Mark and me.

During this period, our phone was ringing off the hook. Call after call, it was fast girls and deep-voiced boys. Half of them were so rude that they wouldn't say hello, how are you doing, or much else to Mark or me. *Where have manners gone?* I wondered. *These young ladies are fearless! They chase these boys like there's no tomorrow.*

I knew good and well that the parents of these young white girls didn't want their daughters chasing this black boy from the 'hood, who was flunking out of school. Then again, maybe times have changed. Today, who cares? And I'm not just referring to the racial issue. More alarming is the lack of parental concern about young ladies who seem more attracted to guys who are headed in the wrong direction, than to nice, responsible young men.

I had to tell Deron and Jeff that too many people were calling them. It was as if they'd given our phone number to everyone in school!

Jeff liked being in high school with his brother. He truly loved Deron and always looked up to him, even when he didn't agree with his brother's behavior. I'm sure that Jeff was often torn between two worlds. Should he listen to Deron, who was so "cool" and who had practically raised him—or should he disappoint his brother by obeying us? Jeff always managed to remain neutral. He never said anything he thought would hurt either of us. Jeff is very intelligent and also is interested in knowing the Lord. But how could he possibly choose between getting close to God and listening to his brother? My prayer is that one day the desire to walk with the Lord will surpass all other desires in his life.

☙

Some days when I picked up the boys from school, Deron would have on other kids' clothes. When I asked him about it, he said they belonged to his friends.

"Deron, where did you get that shirt?" I asked one afternoon.

"Oh, I fell by the swimming pool and got muddy. My friend let me borrow one of his shirts."

"Come on, Deron; it's an indoor pool! Where did the mud come from?"

Deron look dumbfounded, knowing he'd been caught in yet another falsehood. *He doesn't even know how to lie!* I thought.

"I don't know what in the world is wrong with you, that you absolutely cannot tell the truth," I said. I was too furious to argue about it. As he climbed in the car to go home, it crossed my mind that he must have been stealing.

☙

Now that I could no longer trust Deron, I found myself second-guessing him all the time. I also was concerned that Jeff would begin to behave like his older brother. Some mornings I drove by the bus stop just to make sure they were actually going to school. One day when I drove by, Deron had on a completely different outfit from when he had left the house. I called him over to the car and asked him where in the world he was getting the clothes.

"From my friends," he said.

"I can't understand why you have to wear your friends' clothes. And if what you're doing is right, why do you have to sneak around and change?" I asked.

Of course, Deron denied that he was stealing. I think he believed he could outsmart me. But why he would steal was a mystery to me. Both of them had nice things to wear—and more clothes than they'd ever owned before.

ℙ

Mark and I began to argue at great length about the boys. I knew Deron was too much, but I suppose I just wanted them to do better and believed that they could. The situation grew so bad that Deron and Jeff became the topic of all my conversations. It didn't matter whom I was talking to—co-workers, friends in Chicago or Delaware, my sisters, or anyone who knew about my nephews. I loved them dearly, but they were driving me crazy.

I talked to the Lord, fasted and prayed. Mark and I gained a great deal of peace from our weekly Bible study. We knew God had a plan, but we were in the phase of the plan that can often be the most trying—the phase I call the "in-between" stage. At this stage of the game, it's important to know that you're not alone; God is actually carrying you through what sometimes feels like sinking sand.

I literally felt as if I was beginning to break. Most days, I couldn't stop the tears from coming. My heart was so heavy. And I knew that if Deron didn't get his act together, his days of living with us were numbered. I hated to say it, but I was losing hope for him. The lies, the staying out late and the suspected drug use never seemed to end. Mark did not agree with how I was handling Deron; he often pointed out the futility of my empty threats to the boy. *I cannot allow that child to destroy my marriage,* I thought.

But what would happen to Jeff if we sent Deron away? Deron was his brother, his best friend, his hero, his father figure and his soul mate. Basically, Deron was all he had. Knowing that Jeff loved Deron more than anyone in the world, how could I send his brother away?

Yet the decision to send Deron back to Colorado secretly haunted my mind. I had been obsessed with trying to get him to do right, but it was not happening. As my disappointment grew, all I could do was cry. And the more I cried, the bolder he got and the more we encountered the "real" Deron.

It became a daily mystery whether or not Deron would even come home at night. I reported this behavior to our caseworkers in Kansas City and Denver, and they began to ask what I wanted to do. It didn't appear that Deron's behavior was getting any better. I told them I didn't know what to do. *Maybe I do, but I don't have the guts to do it,* I said to myself.

ℙ

One morning I had had it with the lies. I poured my heart out to Deron, telling him to get it together, or he would have to leave. I was dead serious this time; he had pushed me to the very edge. But Deron showed no emotion. I'm sure he figured it was another threat that wouldn't be backed with any action.

Deron had been staying out all day and all night; in fact, he'd been gone for a couple of days. We didn't know where he was. When he finally came home, the young man who brought him back had the nerve to come into my house and tell me that Deron was going to live with him.

"Deron's not going with you anywhere, and get out of my house!"

"Well, you told me if I stayed out not to come back," Deron replied. He went upstairs, as if to get his clothes. I decided to ask his friend a few questions.

"Young man, where are your parents?"

"I live with my dad, and he doesn't care about me," he said. "I do what I want to do."

"Well, maybe you can do that at your house, but things don't work that way here."

This kid was bigger than all of us put together and as tough as he wanted to be. Yet I couldn't help but hear him crying out for love. I called his father that same evening and told him that my nephew had been staying at his house for the last couple of days. I said I didn't know if he was aware of it or not, but that his son was talking about moving Deron in.

The man went ballistic. He said that his son had a lot of friends and that they hung out at his house all the time. He also said that Deron could stay there anytime because we had put him out.

"But why would you take a child's word and not be suspicious?" I asked him.

That's when he started ranting that he'd never had a problem with kids before and that he was on this board and that board. I told him I didn't care what board he was on. If he allowed my nephew to stay in his home, I'd call the police and he'd go straight to jail. I dared him to try me and hung up the phone.

Mark could see that I was burning up with anger and helped me cool down. Fortunately, that man didn't allow Deron back in his home. But Deron's behavior didn't improve any. I wondered what in the world he'd try next.

ℙ

We met with the boy's new caseworker at our home, and she made no bones about what would happen to Deron apart from a serious change in his attitude. She put him on a 30-day trial period, during which he needed to change his ways, or he would have to go back to Colorado.

Mark had absolutely had enough. He was ready for the whole ordeal to be over. While we were sitting at the dining room table with the caseworker, I silently prayed that Mark wouldn't demand that she take the boy away that minute. We agreed to give Deron another chance, monitoring his behavior on a weekly basis. I could see the disappointment in Mark's eyes. Once again Deron had won.

℗

"Deron, we've given you chance after chance," I said after the caseworker had gone. "The reason I haven't given up on you is because I love you. I'll also have you know that the Lord wants us to be obedient of our own free will, and yes, He'll give us several chances, but if we choose not to obey, He will turn us over to our own reprobate minds. That's where we are with you. You don't care what we ask you to do, and you give us no respect. We don't see you getting high, and you aren't doing anything to physically hurt us, but you are very disrespectful."

His only response was that he'd try to do better. I knew then that I was spinning my wheels. It would only be a matter of time.

Deron's friends still called often, and if he didn't answer they would hang up or ask to speak to Jeff as a means of getting to Deron. They knew we had caller I.D., so they decoded their numbers. They were playing games with me, and I knew it. I recognized their voices and told them if they didn't know how to ask for Deron the right way, they should stop calling my house.

My suspicions about Deron grew daily. I wondered about the things he did—and even more about the things I didn't know he did. When the boys first came to live with us, I had told them I would respect their privacy because they weren't little boys anymore. But I also asked for open communication, and I told them that any time I wanted to go in their room, I would do it. I was very clear that I wouldn't treat them any differently than I would my own children.

Because of my suspicion, I started to make spot checks of their room—and not the usual spot check I made every two weeks or so, to air out the stale scent of the room of two teenagers. This time I was checking for drugs and anything else that didn't belong there. I didn't make this a secret. As a matter of fact, I warned the boys about my spot checks.

"If you're as slick as you think you are, then you'd better make sure I don't find anything that smells like trouble," I told them. Still, I checked the room only when I had a strong urge that something wasn't right.

One Saturday while they were away, I looked through their dresser drawers, and there, neatly tucked in Deron's drawer, was a switchblade. It was big enough to kill a man.

I thought I was going to lose it. What in the world was he doing with a knife that size? There were also cassette tapes too filthy for anyone's ears, a cigarette lighter and many other items I had hoped not to find. This was the "real" Deron. What I saw in that drawer was the life he had known in Colorado. Only now it was living under my very own roof.

Then I went through Deron's book bag and found notes from his girlfriend, or so I supposed. The notes were horrible—more appalling than anything I had ever read. *What is this world coming to? The end, for sure,* I thought. The young lady had signed all of her notes, "Love your thug nigga." I wanted to copy the letters and send them to the girl's mother, so that she would know the type of young lady living in her home.

When the boys came in from school that afternoon, they knew I had been in their room. But they didn't say a word about it, and neither did I. In fact, we went the whole weekend without discussing any of it—the switchblade, the lewd music, the disgusting notes and everything else I had found among Deron's things.

Mark and I agreed that if we were to confront Deron, all we'd hear would be lies. And this was not a good weekend to spark another battle with Deron. Mark had recently accepted a new position and was to start a 10-week training program—and he needed to be sharp! Fortunately, the training would be held in Kansas City at a hotel not far from our home. I didn't know if I could handle 10 weeks in the city alone with the boys.

ꝕ

Jeff and I checked Mark into the hotel and returned home to get a good night's rest. There was no sign of Deron that night.

Monday morning, I called Social Services in both Kansas City and Denver, and I told them what I had found. Both agencies expressed fear that our lives were in danger because of the switchblade. I wasn't necessarily afraid for myself since Deron had never acted as if he wanted to hit me. In fact, he never raised his voice at me. If anything, I feared for his life.

Social Services asked that we remove Deron from the home immediately. "But where will he go?" I asked. Already, my mind was spinning out of control. *Oh goodness, it's happening. Why couldn't he just do the right thing?* It felt as if my life had gone into fast-forward. I was torn emotionally, but it was too late for that. The caseworkers were telling me to pull Deron out of school immediately, as he would be going back to Denver the very next day.

Mark was in training, and there was no way for me to contact him. I called my sister, Lisa, who first agreed that this was the best thing to do for Deron. Then she changed her mind.

"Let me see if Carol can take him, so he won't have to go to a foster home," she suggested.

"Lisa, you guys do what you have to do, but I'm expecting Deron to leave tomorrow."

Things were happening way too fast. Feeling panicky, I started to cry. I felt as if I was having to send my very own child away.

ꝑ

On my way to pick up Deron from school, I got another call from the caseworker. She told me they were in the process of locating a shelter for him to be transferred to. It would be a couple of days before they could get him back to Denver. She asked if in the meantime we wanted Deron removed from our home.

"I'd prefer he stay with us until he actually goes," I said.

I also heard from Lisa, who had talked to our oldest sister, Carol. Carol was willing to have Deron come stay with her, but I knew in my heart that this wasn't the best option. My sister lives in one of the smallest towns in

Arkansas and was barely able to care for herself. In reality, Deron would be better off in a shelter.

I called my nephew, Brian, who said he'd be willing to have Deron stay with him for a few days. But I wasn't sure this was the right decision either. *Lord, what am I to do?* I thought.

Finally I reached the school. Silencing my doubts, I walked into the office and calmly informed them that I was there to check Deron out of the school—permanently. Deron met me outside the school office, and we walked together to the parking lot. When we got in the car, I told him that I had been ordered to have him returned to Denver. He looked at me in total disbelief.

"I thought you'd give me another chance!" he exclaimed. That was all he had to say for himself.

"I couldn't, Deron. I had to make a decision."

We drove home in silence.

That afternoon Jeff and I had a serious conversation about his brother leaving. The reason I had struggled so long with my emotions about Deron was that I did not want to separate those boys. I knew what they meant to each other, and to tear them apart would surely break my heart. I was right; when it finally happened, it did just that.

Jeff, who had tried to convince Deron to get his act together on many occasions, decided he would stay with us. I believe Jeff feared that if he were sent with his brother, they would have to go to a foster home or a shelter, and that was not something Jeff wanted to do again.

That evening I was finally able to reach Mark at the hotel. It was hard to find words to express what I was feeling.

"Mark, I spoke with Social Services, and they said Deron will have to return to Denver as soon as possible."

"Really?" he asked.

"Yes. Can you believe it?"

"Well, René, he's really out of hand—and it's to a point where we can't handle him anymore. I know this is hard for you, but we have to do it." I had known he would say that, but I still wasn't ready to hear it. "When is he supposed to leave?" Mark asked.

"In the next couple of days. I had to remove him from school, and somebody has to watch him during the day while I'm at work."

"How's Jeff?"

"He says he wants to stay with us, but I know he's hurt. Deron is all he has." Jeff had never actually said that, but we could tell that in his eyes, Deron was everything. "Mark, the caseworker thought we should have Deron removed from our home. She said he should stay at a local shelter or something. I couldn't handle that, so I said he could keep staying with us until he goes. But I hope he doesn't run away! That's why someone needs to watch him during the day."

"Well, you know I can't. I'm in training."

"I know. I'll figure it out."

Dear God, help me! was all I could pray as I hung up the phone. I really didn't know what I was going to do. The day had flown past as thoughts of Deron's uncertain future had occupied my mind. Now there was so much I needed to process, and so little time to do it.

Jeff and I helped Deron pack his things. Then I told the boys that I wanted them to spend some time together alone. *I wonder if they'll ever see each other again,* I thought to myself as I closed their door behind me.

Going downstairs to fix them dinner, I felt as if Deron was on death row—and we'd just been given word that he would soon be executed. It was my responsibility to make sure he got his favorite meal before meeting his fate tomorrow.

That night we fried chicken, ate apple pie a la mode—and struggled to find the right words to say to one another. I tried to make the evening last as long as possible, wanting to load Deron up with wisdom, much as I had done the first time Mark and I had sent him back to Colorado.

"Deron, understand that everything happens for a reason. You were here for a reason, and now you're leaving for a reason. Please use this time away to seriously consider what you want to do with your life. Please, please, please don't forget to pray. I know you don't understand, but if you pray with a sincere heart, asking God to help you make the right decisions, He will listen to your heart. God will take care of you if you let Him. And the caseworker said if you show improvement—no drugs and passing grades at school—there's a possibility you can come back here. Mark even agreed to your returning if you improve. Mark loves you, Deron. It hurts him that you act as if you don't appreciate our love."

It was hard to tell what Deron was thinking. His face showed no expression, and he hardly said a word.

"Please take advantage of the counseling you will receive," I continued. "As much as I wanted you to, I know it was hard for you to open up and share your feelings with me. But maybe you can talk to others who aren't as close to you as I am. I don't know. I just want you to know I love you, and I want you to choose to do something with your life. Earn your money honestly. It doesn't matter what kind of work you do—just always do your best."

I was rambling—talking uncontrollably as both boys watched me nervously.

"What will you remember most about being here?" I asked Deron.

"I'll probably remember you always talking to me," he replied. "And Mark seemed mad a lot."

"Well, Deron, you really should understand why."

"I know. I do," he said with a smile.

"Just remember, I love you and so does Jesus. This is not the end of the world." I covered his face with kisses—something a teenage boy typically will not tolerate. *What's really going on in his mind? Is he afraid?* I wondered. I used to tell Deron stories about foster-care experiences that terrified even me, hoping it would scare him straight. Was I imagining it, or could I sense fear in the way he smiled at me?

I told the boys they could stay up and talk as late as they wanted to, and I went to bed. As always, I prayed before going to sleep—only this time, I made a special plea for the Lord to take care of Deron. Believe me, it wasn't the first time I'd made such a request. But there's something about pouring your heart out to Him in what seems like the 11th hour. Tears filled my pillow, like a sponge that wouldn't ring dry.

𝓟

"Deron, Jeff, it's time to get up!"

It was morning, and I had awakened slowly, as if from a bad dream I couldn't remember. It felt as if God had rocked me to sleep in the midst of a raging storm.

Jeff was the only one who would go to school this morning. We all got dressed, ate breakfast and I had the boys hug one another. Tears filled Jeff's eyes as he walked down the stairs to catch the bus.

"Deron, you'll have to go with me to work this morning," I said, struggling to hide the catch in my voice. He nodded in agreement. *How can someone so sweet have such a hard time accepting love,* I said to myself. I felt so sorry for Deron. I knew he was carrying around such deep emotional challenges that he just wasn't ready to birth.

On the way to work, I slipped a disk into the CD player—the gospel sounds of Nancy Jackson, who soothed my soul with her words about trusting in the Lord and doing His will. *Cast any doubts and fears away,* she sang. *Lean and depend on the Lord. Why worry? Why cry?*

God is our refuge. I played the song over and over. The words seemed to inject His strength into my own weak and faltering spirit. Deep inside, I knew that Deron would be all right one day. I wanted to shield him from the pain, but I knew that sometimes we don't appreciate the victories if we don't go through the battle.

❦

Around mid-morning, Mark called me on one of his breaks. Knowing I was facing a mountain of work, he volunteered to have Deron stay in his hotel room for the rest of the day. The last thing I wanted was to interrupt Mark's intense training schedule; he needed to score at least a 90 percent on all of his exams.

I drove Deron to the hotel, told him to stay in Mark's room, and asked him to call if he needed anything. As I walked out the door, I could only pray that he wouldn't run away. *He could easily call one of his friends to come pick him up, and we'd probably never see him again,* I thought. But it was a chance I had to take.

When Mark got to the room, Deron was asleep on the couch. Mark had brought him some lunch and told him to make himself at home. My husband later told me that he didn't get to spend much time with Deron since he had to be in class all day, but that for the most part, Deron seemed fine with all that was happening. Mark assumed this was because Deron believed he would have more freedom away from us. Mark assured Deron that he wasn't angry with him—in fact, he agreed with the caseworker that if Deron showed great improvement in the next 90 days, he could come back to Kansas City.

ϕ

On Wednesday we went through a similar routine. I dropped Deron off at Mark's hotel room, while Jeff went to school and I went to work. *What's going on with Social Services?* I wondered all morning. *On Monday, they were in such a big hurry to have Deron return. Yesterday, I didn't even hear from them! If I don't hear from them by noon, I'm going to give them another call.*

That evening, I was scheduled to fly out for a meeting in Florida. I had booked the latest flight available because I wanted to be there when Deron departed. But now the minutes were ticking away, and the pressure to know what would happen to Deron—and when—was almost more than I could bear.

The phone rang; it was the social worker from Colorado. For a moment, it was as if I couldn't hear her words over the drumbeat of my own heart. Sensing my concern, she began to comfort me.

"Everything will be all right," she said. I knew that, but Deron's leaving was a hard pill for me to swallow. Now I knew how my mother must have felt when I encouraged her to give up on Monica because of the horrible things she was doing. Now I could comprehend the impenetrable bond between a mother and her children. I also better understood the love of our heavenly Father toward us, and why He gives us chance after chance. He absolutely loves us.

"So he leaves tonight?" I asked the social worker. "Where will he be going? Um-hum, I see. And how many people are in the shelter? Six females and 10 males? Oh, that's not too bad. How long will he have to stay there? Um-hum, so he'll go to school and everything? Good. Will we be able to have contact with him? Great! Well, thank you for everything. We'll have him at the airport this evening."

Immediately, I called Mark and left a message on his cell phone.

"Mark, Deron is going this evening. He'll be staying in a shelter until they can find him a foster home. I know you have to study, but can you go with Jeff and me to take him to the airport?"

That was all I got out before my voice began to crack.

$$\wp$$

In a way, I felt a sense of relief. Now it was truly over. I finally knew the ending of this chapter of my life.

I picked up Deron from the hotel and told him the news. Then we went home to wait for Jeff. On the way, I asked Deron if he was afraid. When he replied, "Yeah," I thought I was going to wreck the car.

"You are?"

"Yeah, because I don't know where I'm going or who I'll be living with."

"I understand. When I had to leave home for college, I was afraid. I probably felt the same way you're feeling today. On the other hand, I was excited because I had a chance to start all over again. You know what I mean?"

"Yeah, I guess."

"Sooner or later, you're going to have to make up your mind about what you want out of life. I know you know the difference between right and wrong. Deron, learn to make the right choices. As long as you live, you'll always have the option of choosing right or wrong. Always! You're a great young man, and until you learn to break through that brick wall you've built around your emotions, you'll keep trying to suppress your feelings. You are somebody, and what you have to say about who you are plays out in your everyday living.

"I promise to keep in touch with you," I continued, "but I can't do it all by myself. You can call collect anytime, even if only to say hello and hang up. And remember, if the counselors see improvement in your initiative to go to school and stay away from drugs, you'll be allowed to come back. Deron, I've said this so many times before, but if doing drugs and skipping school were good for you, I'd support what you're doing 200 percent. But you've seen how drugs have led your mom down the wrong road!"

I was tired of trying to make him understand. I slipped Nancy into the CD player, and she sang us all the way home.

♥

Jeff rushed into the house after school, as if he already knew that Deron would soon be leaving.

"What's wrong with you, Jeff?"

"Nothing," he replied.

"Why'd you come through the door like that, buddy? You sure you're OK?"

"I'm fine."

I let it go, knowing he wouldn't share with me anyway.

"Jeff, your brother will be leaving this evening."

He looked at me, then quickly eyed Deron, who gave his usual smirk. These two had learned well how to cover their emotions. It made me think about how Jesus had been beaten before they hung Him on the cross. The Bible tells us that He never said a mumbling word. These boys had been beaten as well, and they too never said a mumbling word. No matter how bad the beating, the hunger, the pain of having a mother on drugs, the feelings of being unloved and unwanted, of having no dad, no clothes, no shoes and no place to stay—whatever the circumstances, they never said a mumbling word. *God bless them,* I thought.

"You guys know I have to leave tonight too, for Florida. Deron, make sure you've got all your stuff, and then you and Jeff go ahead and put your things in the car."

They did exactly as I asked.

As they were loading the car, Mark pulled into the driveway. When he came into the house, he looked me in the eye. I couldn't look back; I knew I would break down then and there. It was important that I be strong, or I feared I might back out of the plan. It was taking every ounce of courage I had to do what was right for both Deron

194

and my family.

Mark led us in prayer. Then we gave Deron some cash, climbed in the car and headed for the airport. It was a quiet ride—and much too short. None of us really knew what to feel.

ℙ

We had timed our arrival at the airport so that Deron could get right on the plane. Hanging around, searching for the right words to say—words that could not possibly have mattered at this point—would only have made things worse. We said goodbye, and Deron boarded the plane.

My flight departed 30 minutes after his.

Epilogue

It's been approximately three years since Deron left us. When he returned to Colorado, he stayed in several shelters and two different foster homes before residing in his most recent and permanent foster home. During this time, Deron continued to do the things he did while living with us. His first two foster homes were not as tolerant as we were, so he was removed from their care. Once he even got into trouble with the law.

In the past three years, we've kept up with Deron's whereabouts and well-being. Just when we thought he had reached rock bottom and was on his way to boot camp, our prayers were answered. Deron was taken in by a family new to the foster care system. This couple saw something in Deron and had a desire to try to save him. This family was told not to contact any of Deron's family— not even Mark and me—but when they heard about us, they felt compelled to call and let us know he was alright.

By this time, Deron was almost 18 and could have been dismissed from the system. However, with his foster parents' permission and as long as he attended school, he was allowed to remain in the system and in their home.

While Deron was receiving all the attention, I believe Jeff felt overlooked. As time passed, he missed his brother tremendously and began to be difficult. Soon he opted to return to Colorado on the chance that he might be able to be with his brother. I did everything I could to get him to stay with us; I even painted the horrible picture that he might leave us and still not be reunited with Deron.

But Jeff wanted to take that chance. Eventually, he was placed in the same home as his brother, where he resides today. He is almost 17 as of this writing.

Deron, now age 19, refused to obey house rules, leaving his foster parents no choice but to have him removed from their home. But because of their love for him, they worked tirelessly to get Deron placed in Job Corps. His only remaining alternative was to be sent back to a shelter in Aurora, Colorado.

I was informed that Deron's paperwork for Job Corps would likely not clear before the day he was to leave. Mark and I assisted in clearing a restitution he had with the courts in order to help expedite the paperwork. Then I went into deep prayer, calling on the Hamilton's for support. Deron's future weighed heavily on my heart, and I felt in my spirit that if he were to return to Aurora, he would probably be dismissed from the system and the streets would become his new home. There would be nowhere else for him to go.

When I informed Lisa of Deron's possible return, her response was that maybe Deron and Monica could get an apartment together. I knew then that the Lord needed to intervene right away. I could only envision Deron, Monica and her boyfriend getting high together, hurtling toward the dead-end of drug abuse.

A week after Deron was to have returned to Aurora, I hadn't heard from anyone regarding his whereabouts. Concerned, I decided to call the foster family.

"Oh, I thought you knew Deron was in Job Corps," his foster mom told me. I screamed for joy!

"Mark, he made it to Job Corps! Hallelujah! God is awesome!"

Deron now resides in Utah. He is currently working on his job skills and the completion of his G.E.D. through Job Corps.

My heart still goes out to both the boys. I keep them in my prayers, and I admit that there are moments when I ask myself, Did I do all that I could? Is there anything else I can do now? Will they remember anything I tried to teach them? Do they realize how much I love them? But I believe in my heart that once you've done all you know to do, you have to give your children back to God.

Mark and I are committed to having a continuing role in the boys' lives. We intend to support them, encourage them and pray without ceasing that the Lord will keep them as only He can. We also pray that they will open their hearts and minds to receive His blessings, grow to conquer their past hurts and become good Christian men.

And all thy children shall be taught of the Lord; and great shall be the peace of thy children.

Isaiah 54:13

Deron's Writings

Written In Silence
By Deron

They got me trapped liven a heled life on the edge
Lord knows I been captured as a child
never fed just a hungry skinny penny snacthin
nigga was schooed by drug dealers and hung
out wit thug niggaz Rappin about inner city
life cant have peace on the streetz po babies is
snacthed up Niggaz is sliced up damn what a tragedy
and al I could c 2 get 2 success Bal in the
game and put your mind 2 the test cuz in this Dirty
game there would always be shame By snakes
and Fakes that try 2 cheat you man maintain
and gain knowlegde show them foos
that you can prove them wrong and snacthin colege
a better knowledge

Deron wanted out. He expresses how, since he was a young boy, he was trapped in a life style of "thugging" as his only way of survival. He wants to prove that there is a better way. The answer is college. The challenge is he's trapped.

Was born and raised in hell went from rags to riches
to liven well wonder if my destineys to hell or
rise but time will tell never will I lose hope
wand to be a leader can't be a man if I go for broke
they say as they spoke money makes the man
man makes the money play it smart in your hands
moma always told me she didn't raise no dummy
broke rules in school it was strange and funny
couped out of school started to kick it wit
the dealers on the end of the blocks job was
to hide out ant ride out from the freakin copz
the game didn't stop it only stoped if you got
cought or popped more checkes than the mail
man run inns like federal express liven in crack
houses time was less money tooken to the test
had to wacth yo back couldn't trust nobody
not even blood or cuz had to stay tight

Im on a Rampage meaning strickley business
no causes of snakes and fakes to be my witness
happy as hel as I finish my interview
swiched my style to buck wild thug style continues
mentaly motivated by my moms speech
keep your eyez on the prize a new Queen preach
welfare was another thing she didn't want to commit
no job no pay free rent was the only thing she can
contend wit member the drugs that she lit was higher
than mels momz always in the kicthen tripen
lookin out the window 2 memo tripken its
a bust shh nobody she can trust appeareance
of hilusronations paranoid straight hit the
dust

Deron expresses how he truly felt after he got his job at the grocery store.

Im haven doughtz bout mseld aham to be me
makin It 2 seccess and beh legit was the thang
2 be recently things kind of been tough and
kind of rough I think I had enough Im
taken complements kind of 2 far thinkin I aint
nathen wtthut no money no car and theres nothin
more of beh tru 2 yourself of al stay with
that belief and believe that youl never fail

Deron always talked about how he did not want to forget his past. This was a struggle for him because it scared him to think that he could actually be somebody.

Deron contemplating suicide. Life in his world was too much. Getting high was a way of escape. Along with a pocket full of money.

Im haven suicidal thoughtz but the thing is I cant cope wit it smoken weed seh visions of me dead mentaly thinken wicked and spitted and spitted on the language I communicate verbly slang my mah thang smashing grah into my brah my local hits lyricaly words comih into bits my hot rhymes burn when they lit make a verse or 2 stepin threw stayin h your way what you gona do Im coo for schoo Its ratation but brings education flee from foo and I wont stop head 4 the top til I fal out It wont be comin soon wont be doom or a drop out my goal is to graduate and go to colege

Born h hel 2 liven wel past possesed smoked sess 2 kil stress It was best from beh depressed was careless and fearless never shed no tear never did like beh poor tehn mama I aint happy hear hearh shotz mother scenez ful of powder smoke the dealer man got broke after jacked from slangh dope never loose hope It aint no joke 4 gangbangers 2 represent they pledge life on the edge you better off dead

brought in this world a Kid Bad care aa teen careless
no father figure who can share it 2 be a man
taken liven on my own stand my plan was taken Drama
into my own hand and was depressed getin high was
the only way of bein free was fearless of God
couldnt let evil flee from me calin shots
on the corners serven on wacthed Blocks yelin
1 time dicth the volks dogden buck shots was
only makin a liven emty pocket was mostly broke
moms gon bazerk cuz that white smoke
close 2 hooked gave up Supplies 2 dirty crooks
I couldnt fight was 2 young wqhat was I 2
do but give dirty looks a bad rep look 2
step he was a buddy 2 me laughen at stores
we hit up it was funny 2 me but it was
a tragedy my plot thikens he only showed
love by bein a thug I was gettin lickens
Holerin at females young lookin older who
was skandelez not known they was headed
for cash I was blinded Bardsend Blind
as a Bat lookin at the fact the Black Mac
is Back loves 2 attack my green Stak

207

Deron is expressing how he never would be close to his mom. Now that he was living with Mark and me he felt closer to her. He felt that being with us was probably best for him and his brother. He knew drugs was the cause of the family break up. He too resented the man they all looked up to.

my thoughts was made as a inteligence
little brotha had a reflection of my motha
never 2 think me and her would be close
2 each other and was smothered under as a child
go back and 2 get my way discreet my thug
style even now that im away we are closer
than ever itz better that ever when we
was close together Friction is what brake
us apart drugs was the problem didn't
show affection known it was bad keepin
pain in my hart poor motha was chastise
toward fatha didn't relize how the pain
affected the lady the scence of perfume
comin home telln dumb liez Terry man
it was coo kicken it wit ya drinken
liquor but whatz up bringn drugs in the house I
guess the addiction already hit ya c the evil in
your eye wit ya last picture I handed out my love 2 ya
even though Im with the man above be strong push
and shove much love 2 u Thug

Raised as a getta child lived a thug style
which was moved 2 a better level no
more hel now but was mistakon a life style
I couldn't escape Im just a lean teen leanen
on the foster home scale rate Cash Rules
Everything Around Me Cream A gettin rich
mindless Krazy Adelessons at the age of 16 no pain
no gain no gain no game no shame in this
game I claim 2 entertain the hata brain
jealousy and envy a skralthin casulty 2 fame my
name expose those who hear which is crazy
changed from 2 Kaos before It Baby
hel raise me 2 coo 2 be moved 4 foos
who choose next minute burst 2 curse foos who
snooze the loose my team alers is clockin
wealth inhalen sess no other mess known
Its bad 4 our heath chest

I went from poor 2 liven well
back at home it was hell family joules
was to fast no mail so I started makin
crack celz and all I had was God
to trust packin strapes was a must
loud srens had a brotha thinkin it was
a drug bust and makin chips was my
only mission didn't listen to momz
2 much trippen in the kicthen
and didn't give her much respect
didn't check 2 see if she was oright
drugs causen effect but mom was
coo her #1 rule was a tod moma
didn't raise no foo drug addiction
ran through the whole fam colect cals
of to many problems causen trafic Jam
They said the Goree was a bad name
to claim thats lame cause Deron
Doesn't have any shame in his game
my fam sometimes went from right 2
wrong happy times is gone Life goes on

Dress for sescces Education is the key
God please Don't let evi trick me
pleasure and pain hard core to the brash
misery in the penetentiery niggaz invain
and who can u blame Itz al in the game
was a lost soul my only goal was the
sale the Dope money had me crazy insain
sheets for curtains thats al we had timez was
rough thiN Bad my mad Dad
was Thugg glad to be bad bad 2 the
boneate us out of house and home
and wore cheap chalone to hide al the
fraguence from al the girls he bore
now I got 2 say good bye 2 the bad guy
Today let the past fly by C the future
in my eye and even though Im out
of the hood Im in a safer place
Homez Its al good and if I could
fulfil my dream 2 give the keys
2 my mom 2 the house with ful of supply
and a black leather couch

Maybe he began to see a ray of hope. He expresses how he felt safe living in Kansas. Maybe he would have a future and someday fulfill his dream of buying his mom a home.

Deron knew that enough was enough. He wanted to stay but he allowed the demons within to have victory.

Spontanious combustin 4 which I got evil in me
which my Aunt cant trust irritated dont think
she can take al the lien 2 much in such
a emotional way hopen she would let me stay
cant loose focus keep my head straight and live 2 see
a brighter day which fals in the catagory
where my life 2 suceeded satisfied over greed indeed
and feed off knowledge that my teacher Breath

Another troubled day as I raise hell
Im grounded again a juveline feeln locked
down in the county jail my freedom fail
will there ever be peace shit hell na
Itll always be Hectet on the streetz
Kids gettin beat gangstas at wild wars
gunz possessioned like toys at the child
stores careless little nigga in trouble
skitzafrantic 2 the double headed for
success and then headed for trouble will
I ever stay in a place to face liven in
the past in the burbs gotta stay with my black
raise and closer I can get is to
be a G the Devils never flee getn high
was a way for to be free caught
in suspicion wit my ungulty face gotta
wacth my back from these Snitchen Snakes
tested by foos wacth quick sneaky like
a trick grabbin 4 yo grip keep ya eye
unzipped and grip the pistol poppin clips
shouldn't of pulled the trigga now
you a fearless ass nigga shoud of figga
whos Bigga now yous a cereal killa

Theres a trap 2 this game I play
aint no way 4 me 2 get out put the
stress away and I aint goin back
2 bein broke feeln so much pain had
2 smoke the chronic smoke

The world is cruel but has King 2 rulefity

Im stuck in the dark smoken weed and
still stayin sharp known the weed
It taint healthy in my heart my repu-ta-tion
of a weed smoker my mark is a bad
thing to represent 4 the guardian to
assume the weed smoke and chalk and
straight up partien liven Thug style
Clowns go buck wild crooked smile
fuck fake friends

The bigga the star the harder they fal
Its everybodys eyez on me Im ready to bal
Im tryin to participate in this game I look
forward 2 key 2 success Its gon through
struggin 2 gettin close to loot keep away from miss
hot tail keep the scope out of gettin
mai cus times is hel liven in the jail
cel I had to kick the drug addicted Auntl
aint wit it be strong in the process was lucky
when I did itroad was the weapon if didnt
quit she told me to hit it so now I gotta
keep my head straight away from trouble

Learn how to become a Relative Foster Parent by visiting us at:
www.cantkeepittomyself.com

If you would like to share your experience as a Relative Foster Parent log on at:
www.cantkeepittomyself.com

If you are a Relative Foster Parent and would like to learn more about the Hannah Foundation log on at:
www.hannahcom.com, or call us at 1-866-333-3451

ORDER FORM

Please send Can't Keep it To Myself (Quantity/books) _____
    for $15.00 per copy:

Shipping and Handling Cost: ($3.00 per Book) $_____

Total cost of Book,Shipping and Handling: $_____

(For large quantity of (10) books or more please call
1-866-333-3451 for special discount prices)

Name:_____
        (First)   (Last)

Address:_____(apt/Ste/Floor)_____

City:_____State_____Zip_____

MC/VISA#_____Expires:_____

Check/Money Order $_____Payable to Hannah Communications, Inc.

Daytime Telephone Number: (_____) _____

Signature:_____

Mail to Hannah Communicaions, Inc. P.O. Box 952827 Lake Mary, FL 32746 or
call Hannah Communications at (407) 335-3451 or 1-866-333-3451 to place an order today.